TEXTILES

TEXTILES

SIXTH EDITION

Norma Hollen

Professor Emeritus

Iowa State University

Jane Saddler

Professor Emeritus

Iowa State University

Anna L. Langford

Sara J. Kadolph

Iowa State University

MACMILLAN PUBLISHING COMPANY

New York

Earlier editions copyright © 1955, 1964, 1968, 1973, 1979 by Macmillan
Publishing Co., Inc. Some material reprinted from *Modern Textiles,*
copyright © 1952 by Norma Hollen and Jane Saddler.

Macmillan Publishing Company
866 Third Avenue, New York, New York 10022

Collier Macmillan Canada, Inc.

LIBRARY OF CONGRESS CATALOGING-IN-PUBLICATION DATA
Textiles.

Includes index.
1. Textile industry. 2. Textile fibers. 3. Textile
fabrics. I. Hollen, Norma R. II. Hollen, Norma R.
Textiles.
TS1446.T47 1988   677   87-7052
ISBN 0-02-367530-6

Printing: 1 2 3 4 5 6 7   Year: 8 9 0 1 2 3 4

ISBN 0-02-367530-6

Preface

This text was written for use in an introductory or single college course in textiles. It provides a broad view of the production and utilization of fabrics with emphasis on consumer values and serviceability.

The text is organized in a logical manner. It deals with textile-related terms, fibers, yarns, fabrication methods, finishes, and care. However, each section of the text is complete enough that any order can be used in presenting the material for study.

The sixth edition of *Textiles* has been revised to include new developments in fibers, yarns, fabrication, and finishes. A new chapter on care has been added because of the importance of understanding how to properly clean and store textile products. The book has been reorganized to present more cohesive units and to keep like material together. For example, man-made fibers and fiber modifications have been combined into one chapter. This new chapter comes before any of the man-made fibers. In addition, all woven chapters are grouped together. The two knit chapters follow the woven fabrics, and the finish chapters have been reorganized. An overview of finishing is presented first, followed by aesthetic finishes, special-purpose finishes, flame-retardant finishes and flammability, and dyeing and printing.

We have tried to maintain the strong points of the book, while correcting the weak points. It is not specific to textiles and clothing majors, but is useful for students who will be working with textile products. Interior design and education students will find much useful information in the book.

The book does not require a physical science background. Technical information is presented to assist the student in understanding the material and to provide background information to those students who have had courses in chemistry.

Illustrations assist in understanding the material. Hence, many illustrations are included in the text. Both photographs and drawings are included to represent actual fabrics and production machinery and to clarify details in the fabric and in production of the fabric.

This text will help students to do the following:

- Use textile terminology correctly.
- Know current laws and labeling requirements that regulate textile distribution.
- Understand how production processes affect the characteristics and cost of textile products.
- Appreciate past developments in textiles and recognize the need for future developments.
- Identify fibers, yarns, and fabrics by analysis and some simple procedures.
- Predict fabric performance based on knowledge of fibers, yarns, fabric constructions, and finishes in conjunction with informative labeling.
- Make wise selections of textile products for specific end uses.

- Care for textile products in a satisfactory manner.
- Develop an interest in textiles that will motivate further study.

A student swatch kit has been developed by Textile Fabric Consultants to use in conjunction with this edition of *Textiles*. It is available through Textile Fabric Consultants, P.O. Box 111431, Nashville, TN 37222.

Acknowledgments

We wish to express our appreciation to the following: Darlene Fratzke of Iowa State University, for her assistance with the care chapter and her comments, in general, about the book; Chuck Greiner of the Front Porch Photography Studio, Story City, Iowa, for his help with the photography; Carolyn Kundel, Ruth Glock, Charles Kim, all of Iowa State University, for their suggestions concerning this edition; and Donna Danielson, Iowa State University, for her illustrations.

We also wish to thank our reviewers for their helpful suggestions: Margaret McBurney, Ashland College; Jane Hooper, Wayne State University; Ann Reed, University of Texas at Austin; Alvertia Quesenberry, Ball State University; Doris Beard, California State University; Billie Collier, Ohio University; Christine Ladish, Purdue University; Lucille Golightly, Memphis State University; Ernestine Reeder, Middle Tennessee State University; and Joan Laughlin, University of Nebraska.

Finally, we would like to thank those members of the textile industry who have provided information, diagrams, and photographs.

N. H.
J. S.
A. L. L.
S. J. K.

Contents

1 Introduction 1

2 Textile Fibers and Their Properties 4

3 Selection of Textile Products for Consumer Use 19

4 Cotton 23

5 Flax and Other Natural Cellulosic Fibers 35

6 Wool and Other Animal-Hair Fibers 43

7 Silk 59

8 Introduction to Man-Made Fibers 64

9 Rayon: A Man-Made Cellulosic Fiber 81

10 Acetate: The First Heat-Sensitive Fiber 88

11 Nylon: The First Synthetic Fiber 94

12 Polyester 106

13 Olefin Fibers 119

14 Acrylic, Modacrylic, and Other Vinyl Fibers 125

15 Spandex and Other Elastomeric Fibers 137

16 Special-Use Fibers 143

17 Yarn Classification 151

18 Filament Yarns: Smooth and Bulky 163

19 Spun Yarns and Blends 172

20 Introduction to Fabric Construction 184

21 Weaving and the Loom 189

22 Plain-Weave Fabrics 200

23 Twill- and Satin-Weave Fabrics 209

24 Pile Fabrics 216

25 Structural-Design Fabrics 227

26 Crepe Fabrics 235

27 Lace, Leno Weave, and Narrow Fabrics 240

28 Weft-Knit Fabrics 248

29 Warp-Knit Fabrics 268

30 Film, Foam, Coated Fabrics, Leather, and Fur 279

31 Fiberweb, Net-Like, and Multiplex Structures 286

32 Finishing: An Overview 299

33 Aesthetic Finishes 307

34 Special-Purpose Finishes 317

35 Flame-Retardant Finishes and Flammability 330

36 Dyeing and Printing 335

37 Care of Textile Products 348

Fabric Glossary 359

Index 365

1
Introduction

This chapter begins the detailed study of textiles and the properties they contribute to fabrics, apparel, furnishing, and industrial textiles. A good starting place is the definitions of the component parts of a textile fabric.

Fiber   Any substance, natural or man-made, with a high length-to-width ratio and with suitable characteristics for being processed into a fabric.

Yarn   An assemblage of fibers, twisted or laid together so as to form a continuous strand that can be made into a textile fabric.

Fabric   A planar substance constructed from solutions, fibers, yarns, fabrics, or any combination of these.

Finish   Any process used to convert gray goods (unfinished fabric) into finished fabric.

Food, shelter, and clothing are the basic needs of everyone. Most clothing is made from textiles, and shelters are made more comfortable and attractive by the use of textiles. In fact, some shelters are made from textiles. Textiles are used in the production or processing of many things used in day-to-day living, such as food and manufactured goods.

We are surrounded by textiles from birth to death. We walk on and wear textile products; we sit on fabric-covered chairs and sofas; we sleep on and under fabrics; textiles dry us or keep us dry; they keep us warm and protect us from the sun, fire, and infection. Clothing and furnishing textiles are aesthetically pleasing, and they vary in color, design, and texture. They are also available in a variety of price ranges.

The industrial and medical uses of textiles are many and varied. The automotive industry, one of the largest industries in the United States, uses textiles to make tire cords, upholstery, carpeting, head liners, window runners, seat belts, and shoulder harnesses.

Man has traveled to the moon in a 20-layer, $100,000 space suit that has nylon water-cooled underwear. Life is prolonged by replacing wornout parts of the body with woven- or knitted-fabric parts such as polyester arteries and velour heart valves. Disposable garments are worn by doctors and nurses. Bulletproof vests protect police, hunters, and soldiers, and safety belts make automobile travel less dangerous. Three-dimensional, inflatable "buildings" keep out desert heat and Arctic cold.

This text was written for consumers—not average consumers but educated consumers who, when they purchase textile items, want to know *what* to expect in fabric performance and *why* fabrics perform as they do. Textiles are always changing. They change as fashion changes and as the needs of people change. New developments in production processes also cause changes in textiles, as do government standards for safety, environmental quality, and energy conservation. These changes are discussed, but the bulk of the text is devoted to basic information about textile products, with an emphasis on fibers, yarns, fabric construction, and finishes. All of these elements are interdependent and contribute to the beauty, the durability, the care, and the comfort of fabrics.

Much of the terminology used in the text may be new to students and many facts must be memorized. But to understand textiles in a broad aspect one must first learn the basics. The historical development, the basic concepts, and the new developments in textiles are discussed. Production processes are explained briefly. A knowledge of production should give the student a better understanding of, and appreciation for, the textile industry.

In the United States, the textile industry is a tremendous complex. It includes the natural and man-made fiber producers, spinners, weavers, knitters, throwsters, yarn converters, tufters, fiberweb producers and finishers, machinery makers, and many others. More people are employed in the textile industry than in any other manufacturing industry, over 2 million. Textile products valued at over $40 billion are produced each year by systems that are increasingly being directed by computers. In Japan, at the push of a button, an operator can dye wool fabric in over 2,000 color combinations without flaw or error.

The textile industry has developed from an art-and-craft industry perpetuated by guilds in the early centuries, through the Industrial Revolution in the 18th and 19th centuries, when the emphasis was on mechanization and mass production, to the 20th century, with its emphasis on science and technology.

In this century, man-made fibers were developed and modified textured yarns were created. New fabrications and increased production of knits occurred, and many finishes and sophisticated textile production and marketing systems were developed. These developments have been beneficial to consumers. Man-made fibers and durable press finishes have made many items of clothing "easy care." New developments in textiles have also created some problems for consumers, particularly in the selection of apparel and furnishing textiles. So many items look alike. Knitted fabrics look like woven fabrics and vice versa, vinyl and polyurethane films look like leather, fake furs look like real furs, acrylic- and polyester-fiber fabrics look like wool. The traditional cotton fabrics are now often polyester or polyester/cotton blends.

To make textile selection a bit easier for consumers, textile producers and their associations have set standards and established quality-control programs for many textile products. The federal government has passed laws to protect consumers from unfair trade practices, namely, the Wool Products Labeling Act, the Fur Products Labeling Act, the Textile Fiber Products Identification Act, and the Flammable Fabrics Act. The first three laws are "truth-in-fabrics" legislation and, to be beneficial, some knowledge on the part of the consumer about fibers and furs is required. The Flammable Fabrics Act is protective legislation that prohibits the sale of dangerously flammable apparel and furnishing textiles. The Federal Trade Commission issued the Permanent Care Labeling Rule in 1972 and revised it in 1985. Its purpose is to inform the consumer how to care for fabrics and garments.

Emphasis on energy conservation, environmental quality, noise abatement, health, and safety affect the textile industry as well as other industries. The efforts of the textile industry to meet standards set by the federal government affect the consumer indirectly—by raising prices for merchandise or by limiting the choices available. Energy conservation is being achieved by using less water and faster production methods. Nonpollution of streams and air is being achieved by reducing or eliminating the use of water in many finishing processes and by adding equipment to machines to cleanse and purify the water or air before it is emitted. The Occupational Safety and Health Administration has set standards for noise levels and dust and lint levels that make the mills healthier places in which to work. Much progress has been made in providing flame-resistant fibers and finishes in response to the Consumer Products Safety Commission's implementation of the Flammable Fabrics Act. The CPSC also has commissioned the testing of fabrics and finishes for toxicity and carcinogenicity, and it can request that suspect fabrics be removed from the market.

Textile fabrics can be beautiful, durable, comfortable, and easy care. They can satisfy the needs of all people at all times. Knowing how fabrics are created and used will give a better basis for their selection and an understanding of their limitations.

A knowledge of textiles and their production will result in a more informed selection of a textile product for a particular use. A knowledgeable selection will result in a more-satisfied user.

2

Textile Fibers and Their Properties

It is important to understand the factors influenced by fibers because fibers are the basic unit of most fabrics. Fibers contribute to the aesthetic appearance of fabrics; they influence the durability, comfort, and appearance retention of fabrics; they determine, to a large extent, the care required for fabrics; and they influence the cost of fabrics. Successful textile fibers must be readily available, constantly in supply, and inexpensive. They must have sufficient strength, pliability, length, and cohesiveness to be spun into yarns.

Textile fibers have been used to make cloth for the last 4,000 or 5,000 years. Until 1885, when the first man-made fiber was produced commercially, fibers were obtained from only plants and animals. The fibers most commonly used were wool, flax, cotton, and silk. These four natural fibers continue to be used and enjoyed today, although their economic importance relative to all fibers has decreased.

Textile processes—spinning, weaving, knitting, dyeing, and finishing of fabrics—were developed for the natural fibers. Man-made fibers often resemble the natural fibers.

For example, silk has always been a highly prized fiber because of the smooth, lustrous, soft fabrics made from it; it has always been expensive and comparatively scarce. It was, therefore, logical to try to duplicate silk. Rayon (called artificial silk until 1925) was the first man-made fiber. Rayon was produced in filament length until the early 1930s when an enterprising textile worker discovered that the broken and wasted rayon filaments could be used as staple fiber. Acetate and nylon were also introduced as filaments to be used in silk-like fabrics.

Many man-made fibers were developed in the first half of the 20th century, and from that time onward tremendous advances have been made

in the man-made fiber industry, primarily modifications of the parent fibers to provide the best combination of properties for specific end uses. The man-made fibers most commonly used today in apparel and home-furnishing fabrics include polyester, nylon, olefin, acrylic, rayon, and acetate.

Fiber Properties

Fiber properties contribute to the properties of a fabric. For example, strong fibers contribute to the durability of fabrics; absorbent fibers are good for skin-contact apparel and for towels and diapers; fibers that are self-extinguishing are good for children's sleepwear and protective clothing.

To analyze a fabric in order to predict its performance, start with the fiber. Knowledge of the fiber's properties will help to anticipate the fiber's contribution to the performance of a fabric and the product made from it. Some contributions of fibers are desirable and some are not. Figure 2–1 illustrates this fact by identifying some of the contributions of a low-absorbency fiber.

Fiber properties are determined by the nature of the *physical structure*, the *chemical composition*, and the *molecular arrangement*.

PHYSICAL STRUCTURE

The physical structure, or morphology, of fibers can be identified by observing the fiber through a light, or electron, microscope. In the text, photomicrographs taken by electron microscopes at

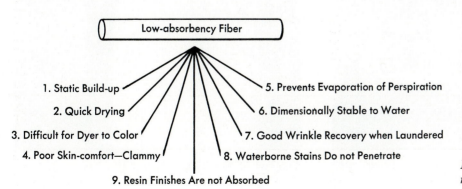

Fig. 2–1 Properties usually related to low absorbency.

magnifications of 250–1,000× will be used to clarify details of the fiber's physical structure.

Length. Fibers are sold by the fiber producer as filament, staple, or filament tow. *Filaments* are long continuous fiber strands of indefinite length, measured in yards or meters. They may be either monofilament (one fiber) or multifilament (a number of filaments). Filaments may be smooth or bulked (crimped in some way), as shown in Figure 2–2. Smooth filaments are used to produce silk-like fabrics; bulked filaments are used in more cotton-like or wool-like fabrics.

Staple fibers are measured in inches or centimeters and range in length from 2–46 cm (¾ of an inch to 18 inches). Staple fibers are shown in Figure 2–3. All the natural fibers except silk are available only in staple form.

The man-made fibers are made into staple form by cutting filament tow into short lengths. *Filament tow* consists of a loose rope or strand of several thousand man-made fibers without a definite twist. Tow is usually crimped after spinning (Figure 2–4).

Diameter, Size, or Denier. Fiber size plays a big part in determining the performance and *hand* of a fabric (how it feels). Large fibers give

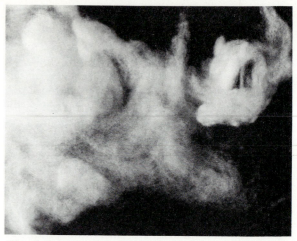

Fig. 2–3 *Man-made staple fiber.*

crispness, roughness, body, and stiffness. Large fibers also resist crushing—a property that is important in carpets, for example. Fine fibers give softness and pliability. Fabrics made with fine fibers will drape more easily.

Natural fibers are subject to growth irregularities and are not uniform in size or development. In natural fibers, fineness is a major factor in determining quality. Fine fibers are of better quality. Fineness is measured in micrometers (a micrometer is 1/1,000 millimeter or 1/25,400 inch).

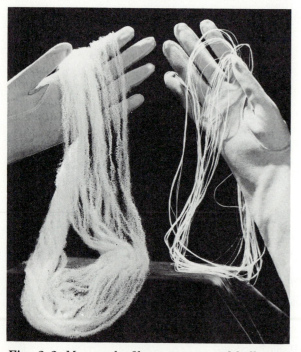

Fig. 2–2 *Man-made filaments: textured-bulk yarn (left); smooth-filament yarn (right).*

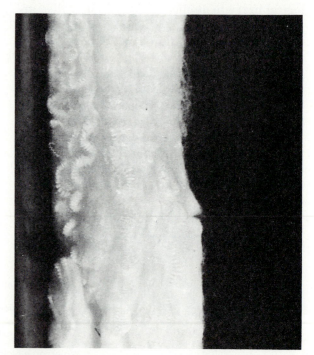

Fig. 2–4 *Filament tow.*

Diameter Range (micrometers)	
Cotton	16–20
Flax	12–16
Wool	10–50
Silk	11–12

In *man-made fibers,* diameter is controlled by the size of the spinneret holes, by stretching or drawing during or after spinning, or by controlling the rate of extrusion of the spinning dope through the spinneret. Man-made fibers can be made uniform in diameter or can be thick-and-thin at regular intervals throughout their length. The fineness of man-made fibers is measured in denier. *Denier* is the weight in grams of 9,000 meters of fiber or yarn. *Tex* is the weight in grams of 1,000 meters of fiber or yarn. Staple fiber is sold by denier and fiber length; filament fiber is sold by the denier of the yarn or tow. Yarn denier can be divided by the number of filaments to give filament denier. For example:

$$\frac{40 \text{ denier yarn}}{20 \text{ filaments}} = 2 \text{ denier per filament.}$$

One to 3 denier corresponds to fine cotton, cashmere, or wool; 5 to 8 denier is similar to average cotton, wool, or alpaca; 15 denier corresponds to carpet wool size.

Apparel fibers range from 1 to 7 denier. Fiber of the same denier is not suitable for all uses. Apparel fibers do not make serviceable carpets and carpet fibers do not make serviceable clothing.

Carpet fibers range in denier from 15 to 24. One of the early mistakes made by the carpet industry was that of using clothing fibers for carpets. These fibers were too soft and pliable, and the carpets did not have good crush resistance. Rayon carpet fiber (1953) was the first fiber made especially for carpets, but it is no longer used in carpeting.

Cross-Sectional Shape. Shape is important in luster, bulk, body, texture, and hand or feel of a fabric. Figure 2–5 shows typical cross-sectional shapes. These shapes may be round, dog-bone, triangular, lobal, bean-shaped, flat, or strawlike.

The natural fibers derive their shape from (1) the way the cellulose is built up during plant growth, (2) the shape of the hair follicle and the formation of protein substances in animals, or (3) the shape of the orifice through which the silk fiber is extruded.

The shape of man-made fibers is controlled by the spinneret and the spinning method. The size, shape, luster, length, and other properties of man-made fibers can be varied by changes in the production process.

Surface Contour. Surface contour is defined as the surface of the fiber along its length. Surface contour may be smooth, serrated, striated, or rough. It is important to the luster, hand, texture, and apparent soiling of the fabric. Figure 2–5 shows some of the differences in the surface contours of different fibers.

Crimp. Crimp may be found in textile materials as fiber crimp or fabric crimp. *Fiber crimp* refers to the waves, bends, twists, coils, or curls along the length of the fiber. Fiber crimp increases cohesiveness, resiliency, resistance to abrasion, stretch, bulk, and warmth. Crimp increases absorbency and skin-contact comfort but reduces luster. Inherent crimp occurs wool. Inherent crimp also exists in an undeveloped state in bicomponent man-made fibers where it is developed in the fabric or the completed garment (such as a sweater) by using suitable solvents or heat treatment.

Fabric crimp refers to the bends due to the interlacing or interlooping of yarns in a fabric. When a yarn is unraveled from a fabric, fabric crimp can easily be seen in the yarn. It also may be visible as the yarn is untwisted into fibers.

Fiber Parts. The natural fibers, except for silk, have three distinct parts: an outer covering, called a *cuticle* or skin; an inner area; and a central core that may be hollow. For example, Figure 4–6 and Figure 6–4 show the structural parts of cotton and wool, respectively.

The man-made fibers are not as complex as those of the natural fibers and there are usually just two parts: a skin and a core.

CHEMICAL COMPOSITION AND MOLECULAR ARRANGEMENT

Fibers are classified into groups by their chemical composition. Fibers with similar chemical

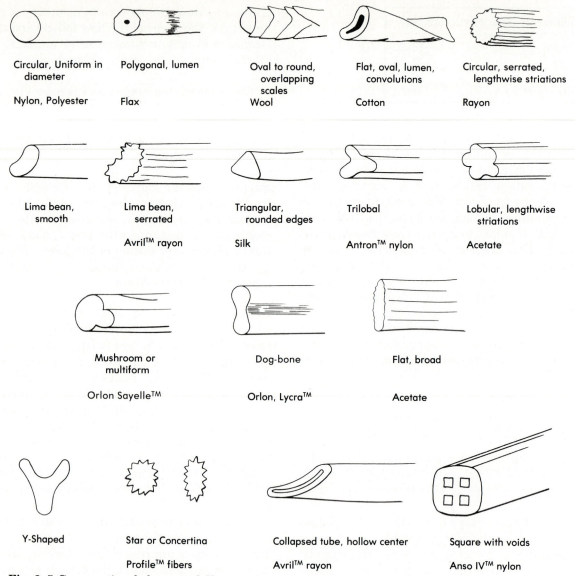

Circular, Uniform in
diameter

Nylon, Polyester

Polygonal, lumen

Flax

Oval to round,
overlapping
scales

Wool

Flat, oval, lumen,
convolutions

Cotton

Circular, serrated,
lengthwise striations

Rayon

Lima bean,
smooth

Lima bean,
serrated

Avril™ rayon

Triangular,
rounded edges

Silk

Trilobal

Antron™ nylon

Lobular, lengthwise
striations

Acetate

Mushroom or
multiform

Orlon Sayelle™

Dog-bone

Orlon, Lycra™

Flat, broad

Acetate

Y-Shaped

Star or Concertina

Profile™ fibers

Collapsed tube, hollow center

Avril™ rayon

Square with voids

Anso IV™ nylon

Fig. 2–5 *Cross-sectional shapes and fiber contours.*

compositions are placed in the same generic group. Fibers in one generic group have different properties from fibers in another group.

Fibers are composed of millions of molecular chains. The length of the chains, which varies just as the length of fibers varies, depends on the number of molecules connected in a chain, and it is described as *degree of polymerization.* Polymerization is the process of joining small molecules—monomers—together to form a long chain or a *polymer.* Long chains indicate a high degree of polymerization and a high degree of

fiber strength. Molecular chains are not visible to the eye or through the optical microscope.

Molecular chains are sometimes described in terms of weight. The molecular weight is a factor in properties such as fiber strength and extensibility. A fiber of longer chains has a higher strength than a fiber of shorter chains of equal weight; the fiber of longer chains is harder to pull apart than the fiber of shorter chains.

Molecular chains have different configurations in fibers. When molecular chains are nearly parallel to the lengthwise axis of the fi-

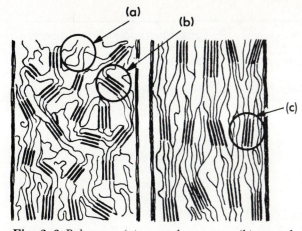

Fig. 2–6 *Polymers: (a) amorphous area; (b) crystalline, but not oriented, area; (c) oriented and crystalline area.*

ber, they are said to be *oriented;* when they are randomly arranged or disordered, they are said to be *amorphous. Crystalline* is the term used to describe fibers that have molecular chains ordered relative to each other, and usually, but not necessarily, parallel to the lengthwise axis of the fiber (Figure 2–6). Different fibers vary in the proportion of oriented, crystalline, and amorphous regions.

The polymers in man-made fibers are in a random, unoriented state when extruded from the spinneret. *Stretching,* or *drawing,* increases their crystallinity and orients them, reduces their diameter, and packs their molecules together (Figure 2–7). Physical properties of the fiber—such as strength, elongation, moisture absorption, abrasion resistance, and receptivity of the fiber to dyes—are related to the amount of crystallinity and orientation.

Molecular chains are held to one another by *cross links* or by intermolecular forces called *hydrogen bonds* and *van der Waals forces.* The forces are similar to the attraction of a magnet for a piece of iron. The closer the chains are together, the stronger the bonds are. Hydrogen bonding is the attraction of positive hydrogen atoms of one chain for negative oxygen or nitrogen atoms of an adjacent chain. Van der Waals forces are similar but weaker bonds. It is in the crystalline area that hydrogen bonding and van

Unstretched or Undrawn   Stretched or Drawn

Fig. 2–7 *Before and after drawing the fiber.*

der Waals forces occur. Cross links and intermolecular forces help make crystalline polymers stronger than amorphous polymers.

Serviceability

Textile serviceability includes the five concepts of aesthetics, durability, comfort, appearance retention, and care. Each concept will be discussed in terms of properties that affect it. For example, the aesthetic properties of luster, drape, texture, and hand, as they relate to apparel and furnishing fabrics, will be defined and discussed.

A note to students: Learn the definitions of the properties. Use the tables as you study each fiber in subsequent chapters to see how that particular fiber compares with other fibers. During this process, evaluate your experience with fabrics made of that fiber and try to understand why they performed the way they did. Once you understand the information, you will remember it and use it now and in future years.

AESTHETIC PROPERTIES

A textile product should be attractive and appropriate in appearance for its end use. Aesthetic properties relate to the way the senses of touch and sight perceive the textile. In evaluating the aesthetics of a textile item, the consumer usually determines whether the item is attractive and appropriate in appearance for its end use.

Luster results from the way light is reflected by a fabric's surface. It is observed by the eye. Shiny or bright fabrics reflect light and are used for certain end uses. Lustrous fabrics reflect a fair amount of light and are used in formal apparel and furnishings. Matte, or dull, fabrics reflect little light and are used most frequently for less-formal looks in apparel and furnishings. Silk fabrics are usually lustrous. Cotton and wool fabrics are usually matte. The luster of man-made fibers can be varied during manufacturing to result in bright, semibright, or matte fibers. Yarn structure, finish, and fabric structure may enhance or decrease the luster of fibers.

Fiber Property Chart

Fiber Property	Is Due to	Contributes to Fabric Property
Abrasion resistance is the ability of a fiber to withstand the rubbing or abrasion it gets in everyday use.	Tough outer layer, scales, or skin Fiber toughness Flexible molecular chains	Durability Abrasion resistance Resistance to splitting
Absorbency or moisture regain is the percentage of moisture a bone-dry fiber will absorb from the air under standard conditions of temperature and moisture.	Hydroxyl groups Amorphous areas	Comfort, warmth, water repellency, absorbency, static buildup Dyeability, spotting Shrinkage Wrinkle resistance
Aging resistance	Chemical structure	Storing of fabrics
Allergenic potential is the ability to cause some physical reaction, such as skin irritation or watery eyes.	Chemical composition, additives	Comfort
Chemical reactivity is the effect of acids, alkali, oxidizing agents, solvents, or other chemicals.	Polar groups of molecules Chemical composition	Care required in cleaning—bleaching, ability to take acid or alkali finishes
Cohesiveness is the ability of fibers to cling together during spinning.	Crimp or twists, surface properties	Resistance to raveling Resistance to yarn slippage
Cover is the ability to occupy space for concealment or protection.	Crimp, curl, or twist Cross-sectional shape	Warmth in fabric Cost—less fiber needed
Creep is delayed elasticity. Recovers gradually from strain.	Lack of side chains, cross links, strong bonds; poor orientation	Streak dyeing and shiners in fabric
Density—see *Specific gravity.*		
Dimensional stability is the ability to retain a given size and shape through use and care.	Physical structure, chemical structure, coatings	Shrinkage, growth, care, appearance, durability
Drape is the manner in which a fabric falls or hangs over a three-dimensional form.	Fiber size and stiffness	Appearance
Dyeability is the fibers' receptivity to coloration by dyes; dye affinity.	Amorphous areas and dye sites, chemical structure	Aesthetics and colorfastness
Elastic recovery is the ability of fibers to recover from strain.	Chemical and molecular structure: side chains, cross linkages, strong bonds	Processability of fabrics Resiliency Delayed elasticity or creep
Elasticity is another term for elastic recovery.		
Electrical conductivity is the ability to transfer electrical charges.	Chemical structure: polar groups	Poor conductivity causes fabric to cling to the body, electric shocks
Elongation is the ability to be stretched, extended, or lengthened. Varies at different temperatures and when wet or dry.	Fiber crimp Molecular structure: molecular crimp orientation	Increases tear strength Reduces brittleness Provides "give"
Feltability refers to the ability of fibers to mat together.	Scale structure of wool	Fabrics can be made directly from fibers Special care required during washing
Flammability is the ability to ignite and burn.	Chemical composition	Fabrics burn
Flexibility is the ability to bend repeatedly without breaking.	Flexible molecular chain	Stiffness, drape, comfort

Fiber Property Chart *(continued)*

Fiber Property	*Is Due to*	*Contributes to Fabric Property*
Hand is the way a fiber feels: silky, harsh, soft, crisp, dry.	Cross-sectional shape, surface properties, crimp, diameter, length	Hand of fabric
Heat conductivity is the ability to conduct heat away from the body.	Crimp, chemical composition Cross-sectional shape	Warmth
Heat sensitivity is the ability to soften, melt, or shrink when subjected to heat.	Chemical and molecular structure Fewer intermolecular forces and cross links	Determine safe washing and ironing temperatures
Hydrophilic, hygroscopic—see *Absorbency.*		
Loft, or compressional resiliency, is the ability to spring back to original thickness after being compressed.	Fiber crimp Stiffness	Springiness, good cover Resistance to flattening
Luster is the light reflected from a surface. More subdued than shine; light rays are broken up.	Smoothness Fiber length Flat or lobal shape Additives	Luster 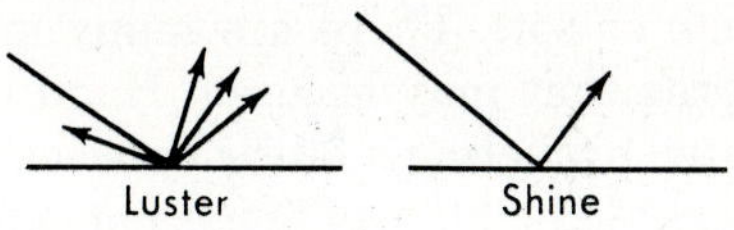
Mildew resistance	Low absorption	Care during storage
Moth resistance	Molecule has no sulfur	Care during storage
Pilling is the balling up of fiber ends on the surface of fabrics.	Fiber strength High molecular weight	Pilling Unsightly appearance
Resiliency is the ability to return to original shape after bending, twisting, compressing, or a combination of the deformations.	Molecular structure: side chains, cross linkages, strong bonds	Wrinkle recovery, crease retention, appearance, care
Specific gravity and density are measures of the weight of a fiber. Density is the weight in grams per cubic centimeter, and specific gravity is the ratio of the mass of the fiber to an equal volume of water at 4°C.	Molecular weight and structure	Warmth without weight Loftiness—full and light Buoyancy to fabric
Stiffness or rigidity is the opposite of flexibility. It is the resistance to bending or creasing.	Chemical and molecular structure	Body of fabric Resistance to insertion of yarn twist
Strength is defined as the ability to resist stress and is expressed as *tensile strength* (pounds per square inch) or as *tenacity* (grams per denier).	Molecular structure—orientation, crystallinity, degree of polymerization	Durability, tear strength, sagging, pilling Sheerer fabrics possible with stronger fine fibers
Sunlight resistance is the ability to withstand degradation from direct sunlight.	Chemical composition Additives	Durability of curtains and draperies, outdoor furniture, outdoor carpeting
Texture is the nature of the fiber surface.	Physical structure	Luster, appearance
Translucence is the ability of a fiber, yarn, or fabric to allow light to pass through the structure.	Physical and chemical structure	Appearance
Wicking is the ability of a fiber to transfer moisture along its surface.	Chemical and physical composition of outer surface	Makes fabrics comfortable

(Diagram labels: Luster   Shine)

Drape is the way a fabric falls over a three-dimensional form like a body or table. Fabric may be soft and free-flowing like chiffon, or it may fall in graceful folds like a percale, or it may be stiff and heavy like bridal satin. Fibers influence drape to a degree, but yarns and fabric structure may be more important in determining drape.

Texture describes the nature of the fabric surface. It is identified by both visual and tactile senses. Fabrics may have a smooth or rough texture. Natural fibers tend to give a fabric more texture than man-made fibers because of their inherent variations. Yarns, finishes, and fabric structure greatly affect the texture of a fabric.

Hand is the way a fabric feels to the touch. Fabrics may feel warm or cool, bulky or thin, slick or soft. There are many more descriptive words that may be used. Hand usually is evaluated by feeling a fabric between the fingers and thumb. The hand of fabric may also be evaluated by the way it feels against the skin. Subjective evaluation determines the fabric's acceptability for a particular end use; however, some researchers are developing an objective means of assessing hand.

DURABILITY PROPERTIES

A durable textile product should last an adequate period of time for its end use. Durability properties can be tested in the laboratory, but lab results do not always accurately predict performance during actual use.

Abrasion resistance is the ability of a fabric to withstand the rubbing it gets in use. Abrasion can occur when the fabric is fairly flat—as when the knees of jeans scrape along a cement sidewalk. Edge abrasion can occur when the fabric is folded—as when the bottom of a drapery fabric rubs against a carpet. Flex abrasion can occur when the fabric is moving and bending—as in shoelaces that wear out where they are laced through the shoe. *Flexibility,* the ability to bend repeatedly without breaking, is a very important property that is related to abrasion resistance.

Tenacity, or tensile strength, is the ability of a fabric to withstand a pulling force. Tenacity for a fiber is the force, in grams per denier or tex, required to break the fiber. The tenacity of a wet fiber frequently differs from the tenacity of that same fiber when it is dry. Although the fabric strength depends, to a large degree, on

Abrasion Resistance

Fiber	Rating
Nylon	Excellent
Olefin	
Polyester	
Spandex	
Flax	
Acrylics	to
Cotton	
Silk	
Wool*	
Rayon	
Acetate	
Glass	Poor

*Varies with coarseness of fiber.

Fiber Strength

Fiber*	Tenacity (grams/denier)	
	Dry	Wet
Natural Fibers		
Cotton	3.5–4.0	4.5–5.0
Flax	3.5–5.0	6.5
Silk	4.5	2.8–4.0
Wool	1.5	1.0
Man-Made Fibers		
Acetate	1.2–1.4	1.0–1.3
Acrylic	2.0–3.6	1.8–3.5
Aramid (staple Nomey)	4.0–5.3	4.0–5.0
Flurocarbon	0.8–1.4	same
Glass (multifilament)	9.6	6.7
Modacrylic	1.7–3.5	1.5–2.4
Novoloid	1.5–2.5	1.3–2.3
Nylon 6 (staple)	3.5–7.2	same
Nylon 66 (staple)	2.9–7.2	2.6–5.4
Olefin	3.5–8.0	same
PBI	2.6–3.0	2.1–2.5
Polyester (staple)	2.4–5.5	same
Rayon (Regular)	0.7–2.6	0.4–1.4
Rubber	0.34	same
Saran	1.4–2.4	same
Spandex	0.6–0.9	same
Sulfar	3.0–3.5	same
Vinyon	0.7–1.0	same

*For fibers that are available in several lengths and modifications, the values are for staple fibers with unmodified cross-sections.
Source: Textile World, 1986.

fiber strength, yarn and fabric structure may be varied to yield stronger or weaker fabrics made from the same fibers. Strength may also be measured by how much force it takes to rip the fabric (tearing strength) or to rupture the fabric (bursting strength).

Elongation refers to the degree to which a fiber may be stretched without breaking. It is measured as percent elongation at break. It should be considered in relation to elasticity.

COMFORT PROPERTIES

A textile product should be comfortable as it is worn or used. This is primarily a matter of personal preference and individual perception of comfort under different climatic conditions and degrees of physical activity. Comfort is a complex area and is dependent on characteristics such as absorbency, thermal retention, density, and elongation.

Absorbency is the ability of a fiber to take up moisture from the body or from the environment. It is measured as moisture regain where the moisture in the material is expressed as a percent of the weight of the moisture-free material. Absorbency is also related to static build-up. *Hydrophilic* fibers absorb moisture readily. *Hydrophobic* fibers have little or no absorbency. *Hygroscopic* fibers absorb moisture from the air.

Thermal retention is the ability of a fabric to hold heat. For apparel, it is important for a person to feel comfortably warm in cool weather or comfortably cool in hot weather. A low level of thermal retention is favored in hot weather. This property accounts for the fact that most people dress and use textiles differently in summer and winter weather. Yarn and fabric structure and layering of fabrics are all very important in enhancing this property.

Density is a measure of fiber weight in weight per unit volume. Lighter-weight fibers can be made into thick fabrics that are more comfortable than heavier-weight fibers made into heavy, thick fabrics.

Elongation: Breaking

Fiber*	% Elongation at Break	
	Standard**	Wet
Natural Fibers		
Cotton	3–7	9.5
Flax	2.0	2.2
Silk	20	30
Wool	25	35
Man-Made Fibers		
Acetate	25	35
Acrylic	20	26
Aramid (Nomex)	22	20
Glass	3.1	2.2
Modacrylic	30–60	same
Nylon (6,6)	16	18
Olefin	10–45	same
PBI	25–30	26–32
Polyester staple	40–45	same
Rayon	15	20
Rubber	500	same
Spandex	400–700	same
Sulfar	35–40	same

Note: A minimum of 10% is desirable for ease in textile processing.

*For fibers that are available in several lengths and modifications, the values are for staple fibers with unmodified cross-sections.
**Standard condition: 65 percent relative humidity, 70°F.

Absorbency

Fiber	Moisture Regain*
Natural Fibers	
Cotton	7–11
Flax	12
Silk	11
Wool	13–18
Man-Made Fibers	
Acetate	6.0
Acrylic	1.0–2.5
Aramid	6.5
Glass	0.0
Modacrylic	2.0–4.0
Nylon (6,6)	4.0–4.5
Olefin	0.01–0.1
PBI	15
Polyester	0.4–0.8
Rayon	13
Saran	0.1
Spandex	1.3
Sulfar	0.6

*Moisture regain is expressed as a percentage of the moisture-free weight at 70°F and 65 percent relative humidity.

Thermal Properties

Fiber	Melting Point °F	Melting Point °C	Softening Sticking Point °F	Softening Sticking Point °C	Safe Ironing Temperature* °F	Safe Ironing Temperature* °C
Natural Fibers						
Cotton	Does not melt				425	218
Flax	Does not melt				450	232
Silk	Does not melt				300	149
Wool	Does not melt				300	149
Man-Made Fibers						
Acetate	500	230	350–375	184	350	177
Acrylic			430–450	204–254	300	149–176
Aramid	Does not melt—Carbonizes above 700°F (Nomex) or 900°F (Kevlar)				Do not iron	
Glass	2,720		1,560	1,778	Do not iron	
Modacrylic	Does not melt				200–250	93–121
Nylon 6	419–430		340	171	300	149
Nylon 66	480–500		445	229	350	177
Olefin	320–350		285–330	127	150	66
PBI	Does not melt		Decomposes at 860°F			
Polyester PET	482		440–445	238	325	163
Polyester PCDT	478–490		470	254	350	177
Rayon	Does not melt				375	191
Saran	350	177	240	115	Do not iron	
Spandex	446	230	420	175	300	149

*Lowest setting on irons: 185–225°F

APPEARANCE RETENTION PROPERTIES

A textile product shold retain its original appearance during wear and care.

Resiliency is the ability of a fabric to return to its original shape after bending, twisting, or crushing. A common test is to crush a fabric in the hand and watch how it responds when the hand is opened. A resilient fabric will spring back; it is wrinkle resistant if it does not wrinkle easily. It has good wrinkle recovery if it returns to its original look after having been wrinkled.

Dimensional stability can be defined as the ability of a fabric to retain a given size and shape through use and care. Dimensional stability is a desireable characteristic that includes the properties of shrinkage resistance and elastic recovery. *Shrinkage resistance* is the ability of a fabric to retain a given size after care. It is related to the fabric's reaction to water or heat. A fabric that shrinks is smaller after care. In addition to a poor appearance, it will have a poor fit.

Elasticity or *elastic recovery* is the ability of a fabric to return to its original dimensions after elongation. It is measured as the percent of return to its original length. Since recovery varies with the amount of elongation, as well as with the length of time the fabric is stretched, the measurement identifies the percent elongation, or stretch, and the recovery. Fabrics with poor elastic recovery tend to stretch out of shape. Fabrics with good elastic recovery usually exhibit good resiliency.

CARE PROPERTIES

Any treatments that are required to maintain the new look of a textile product during use, cleaning, or storage are referred to as care. Improper care procedures can result in items that are unattractive, not as durable as expected, and uncomfortable. The way fibers react to water, chemicals, and heat in ironing and drying will be discussed in each fiber chapter. Any special requirements of storage will also be discussed.

As students learn these basic properties and

Density and Specific Gravity*

Fibers	Density (g/cc)
Natural Fibers	
Cotton	1.52
Flax	1.52
Silk	1.25
Wool	1.32
Man-Made Fibers	
Acetate	1.32
Acrylic	1.0–2.5
Aramid	1.38–1.44
Flurocarbon	0.8–2.2
Glass	2.48–2.54
Modacrylic	1.35
Novoloid	1.25
Nylon	1.13–1.14
Olefin	0.90–0.91
PBI	1.43
Polyester	1.34–1.39
Rayon	1.48–1.54
Saran	1.70
Spandex	1.20–1.25
Sulfar	1.37

*Ratio of weight of a given volume of fiber to an equal volume of water.

remember the effect of other related properties on each serviceability concept, their understanding of the performance of each fiber will

Elastic Recovery

Fiber	% Recovery from 3% Stretch*
Natural Fibers	
Cotton	75
Flax	65
Silk	90
Wool	99
Man-Made Fibers	
Acetate	58 (at 4%)
Acrylic	92
Aramid	100
Glass	100
Modacrylic	88
Nylon	82–89
Olefin	92–98 (at 5%)
Polyester	76
Rayon	80 (at 2%)
Spandex	99 (at 50%)
Sulfar	96 (at 5%)

*Unless otherwise noted.

increase. Students are strongly encouraged to study the performance of each fiber for each of these main concepts.

FIBER PROPERTY CHARTS

The fibers within each generic family have individual differences. These differences are not reflected in the charts shown here, except in a few specific instances. The figures are averages, or medians, and are intended as a general characterization of each generic group. The figures were compiled from the following sources:

Charts: Man-Made Fiber Chart, *Textile World* (August 1986).
Properties of the Man-Made Fibers, *Textile Industries* (1971/1972).
Man-Made Fiber Deskbook, *Modern Textiles* (March 1983).

Bulletins: Textile Fibers and Their Properties, AATCC Council on Technology 1977
Technical Bulletins, Du Pont, Celanese, and Monsanto.
Man-Made Fiber Fact Book, Man-Made Fiber Producers Association, Inc. 1978.

Effect of Acids

Fiber	Effect
Natural Fibers	
Cotton	Harmed
Flax	Harmed
Silk	Harmed by strong mineral acids, resistant to organic acids
Wool	Resistant
Man-Made Fibers	
Acetate	Unaffected by weak acids
Acrylic	Resistant to most
Aramid	Resistant to most
Glass	Resistant
Modacrylic	Resistant to most
Nylon	Harmed, especially nylon 6
Olefin	Resistant
PBI	Resistant
Polyester	Resistant
Rayon	Harmed
Spandex	Resistant
Sulfar	Resistant

Sunlight Resistance

Fiber	Rating
Glass	Excellent
Acrylic	
Modacrylic	
Polyester	
Sulfar	
Flax	
Cotton	to
Rayon	
PBI	
Triacetate	
Acetate	
Olefin	
Nylon	
Wool	
Silk	Poor

Fiber Identification

The procedure for identification of the fiber content of a fabric depends on the nature of the sample, the experience of the analyst, and the facilities available. Because laws require the fiber content of apparel and furnishing textiles to be indicated on the label, the consumer may

Effect of Alkali

Fiber	Effect
Natural Fibers	
Cotton	Resistant
Flax	Resistant
Silk	Damaged
Wool	Harmed
Man-Made Fibers	
Acetate	Little effect
Acrylic	Resistant to weak
Aramid	Resistant
Glass	Resistant
Modacrylic	Resistant
Nylon	Resistant
Olefin	Highly resistant
PBI	Resistant to most
Polyester	Degraded by strong
Rayon	Resistant to weak
Spandex	Resistant
Sulfar	Resistant

only need to look for identification labels. If the consumer wishes to confirm or check the information on the label, burning and some simple solubility tests may be used.

VISUAL INSPECTION

Visual inspection of a fabric for appearance and hand is always the first step in fiber identification. It is no longer possible to make an identification of the fiber content by the appearance and hand alone because man-made fibers can be made to resemble natural fibers and frequently resemble other man-made fibers. However, observation of the following characteristics is helpful.

1. Length of fiber. Untwist the yarn to determine length. Any fiber can be made in staple length, but not all fibers can be filament. For example, cotton and wool are always staple.

2. Luster or lack of luster.

3. Body, texture, hand—soft-to-hard, rough-to-smooth, warm-to-cool, or stiff-to-flexible.

BURNING TEST

The burning test can be used to identify the general chemical composition, such as cellulose, protein, mineral, or man-made polymers, and thus identify the group to which a fiber belongs. *Blends cannot be identified by the burning test.* If visual inspection is used along with the burning test, fiber identification can be carried further. For example, if the sample is cellulose and also filament, it is rayon; but if it is staple, a positive identification for a specific cellulosic fiber cannot be made.

The following are general directions for the burning test:

1. Ravel out and test several yarns from each direction of the fabric to see if they have the same fiber content. Differences in luster, twist, and color will indicate that there might be two or more generic fibers in the fabric.

2. Hold the yarn horizontally, as shown in Figure 2–8. Use tweezers to protect fingers. Feed the yarns slowly into the edge of the flame from the alcohol lamp and observe what happens. Repeat this several times to check results.

Identification by Burning

Fibers	When Approaching Flame	When in Flame	After Removal from Flame	Ash	Odor
Cellulose Cotton Flax Rayon	Does not fuse or shrink from flame	Burns	Continues to burn, afterglow	Gray, feathery, smooth edge	Burning paper
Protein Silk Wool	Curls away from flame	Burns slowly	Usually self-extinguishing	Crushable black ash	Burning hair
Acetate	Fuses away from flame	Burns with melting	Continues to burn and melt	Brittle black hard bead	Acrid
Acrylic	Fuses away from flame	Burns with melting	Continues to burn and melt	Brittle black hard bead	—
Glass		Does not burn			
Modacrylic	Fuses away from flame	Burns very slowly with melting	Self-extinguishing, white smoke	Brittle black hard bead	—
Nylon	Fuses and shrinks away from flame	Burns slowly with melting	Usually self-extinguishing	Hard gray or tan bead	Celery-like
Olefin	Fuses and shrinks away from flame	Burns with melting	Usually self-extinguishing	Hard tan bead	—
Polyester	Fuses and shrinks away from flame	Burns slowly with melting; black smoke	Usually self-extinguishing	Hard black bead	Sweetish odor
Saran	Fuses and shrinks away from flame	Burns very slowly with melting	Self-extinguishing	Hard black bead	—
Spandex	Fuses but does not shrink from flame	Burns with melting	Continues to burn with melting	Soft black ash	—

Fig. 2–8 Fiber identification by the burning test.

MICROSCOPY

A knowledge of fiber structure, obtained by seeing the fibers through the microscope and observing some of the differences among fibers in each group, is of help in understanding fibers and fabric behavior.

Positive identification of most of the natural fibers can be made by using this test. The man-made fibers are more difficult to identify because some of them look alike and their appearance may be changed by variations in the manufacturing process. Positive identification of the man-made fibers by this means is rather limited. Cross-sectional appearance is helpful if more careful examination is desired.

Longitudinal and cross-sectional photomicrographs of individual fibers are included in the fiber chapters. These may be used for reference when checking unknown fibers.

Solubility Tests

Solvent	Fiber Solubility
1. Acetic acid (100%) 20°C	Acetate
2. Acetone, 100%, 20°C	Acetate, modacrylic, vinyon
3. Hydrochloric acid, 20% concentration, 1.096 density, 20°C	Nylon 6, nylon 6,6, vinal
4. Sodium hypochlorite solution (5%) 20°C	Silk and wool (silk dissolves in 70% sulfuric acid at 38°C), azlon
5. Xylene (meta), (100%) 139°C	Olefin and saran (saran dissolves in 1.4 dioxane at 101°C; olefin is not soluble), vinyon
6. Dimethyl formamide, (100%) 90°C	Spandex, modacrylic, acrylic, acetate, vinyon
7. Sulfuric acid, 70% concentration, 38°C	Cotton, flax, rayon, nylon, acetate, silk
8. Cresol (meta), (100%) 139°C	Polyester, nylon, acetate

The following are directions for using the microscope:

1. Clean the lens, slide, and cover glass.

2. Place a drop of distilled water or glycerine on the slide.

3. Untwist a yarn and place the loosened fibers on the slide. Cover with the cover glass and press down to eliminate air bubbles.

4. Place the slide on the stage of the microscope and then focus with low power first. If the fibers have not been well separated, it will be difficult to focus on a single fiber.

5. If a fabric contains two or more fiber types, test each fiber and both warp and filling yarns.

SOLUBILITY TESTS

Solubility tests are used to identify the man-made fibers by generic class and to confirm identification of natural fibers. Two household tests, the alkali test for wool and the acetone test for acetate, are described on pages 54 and 91, respectively.

In using the tests, the specimen should be placed in the liquid in the order listed. The specimen should be stirred for 5 minutes and the effect noted. Fiber, yarns, or small pieces of fabric may be used. The liquids are hazardous and should be handled with care. Chemical laboratory exhaust hoods, gloves, aprons, and goggles should be used.

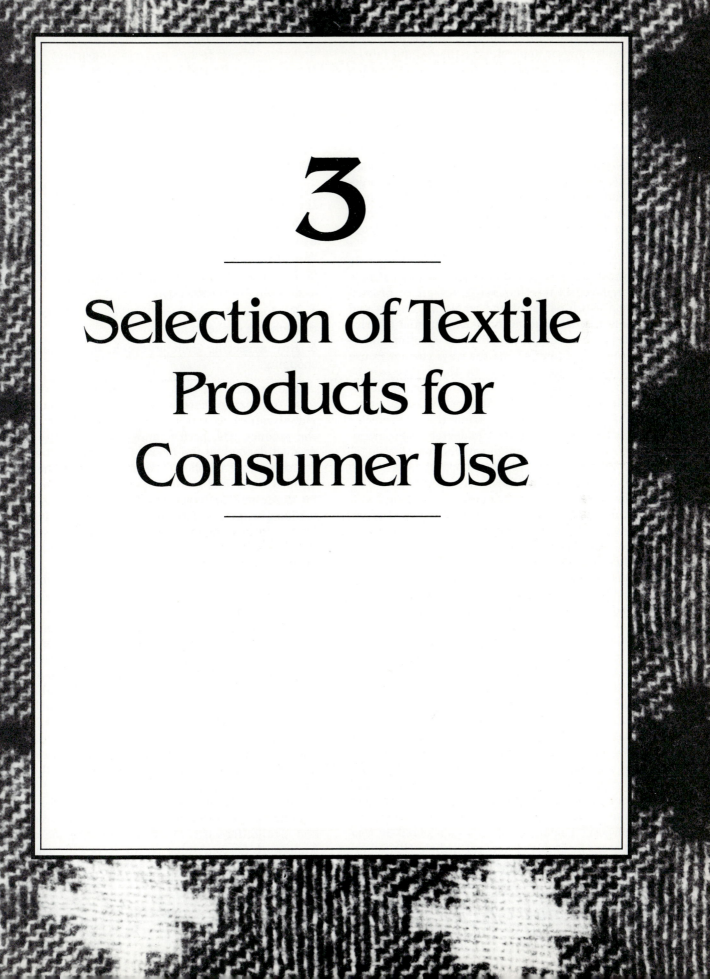

3

Selection of Textile Products for Consumer Use

Many textiles are used as a part of daily life. Ready-to-wear apparel, over-the-counter fabrics that will be sewn into apparel or furnishing items, and home furnishings are chosen by consumers for their use.

The selection of textile products is a personal decision based on many factors, including current fashion, lifestyle, income, sex, and age. The selection is influenced by aesthetic, psychological, sociological, and economic aspects. The decision to buy a product may be rational or it may be impulsive. This chapter provides a framework to help consumers make rational decisions about textile purchases.

This same framework is very useful for people whose jobs are related to textile products. People employed in merchandising, design, or production—such as retail and wholesale buyers and salespersons, and fabric, garment, and interior designers—can all benefit from a better understanding of textiles and the ways customers use these products. Persons in these jobs can be called pre-selectors. What they select determines what the consumer has available to purchase. Hence, the decisions the pre-selector makes influence, to a large degree, the consumer's choice and ultimate satisfaction.

Before consumers start shopping for a textile product, they will have already decided the item for which they are shopping. They should also think through pertinent factors: Who will be using the item? How will it be used? When will it be used? How long will it need to last? Usually this thinking is in terms of what the item will be used for, or, in other words, the end use.

The end use that is identified affects the subsequent selection. Is the coat to be worn by a college student or for school and play by a rambunctious nine-year-old? Will the fabric be made into a pair of slacks for a teenager or for an elderly person in a nursing home? Are the sheets and bedspread for college use, where they must serve both living and sleeping functions, or are they for the master bedroom of a carefully decorated model home? Is the suit to be worn in the summer for casual wear or will it be worn at work throughout the fall, winter, and spring?

With the end use clearly in mind, additional factors need to be considered. What factors are important in making the item serviceable for its purpose? Factors frequently considered by consumers for items of apparel include the following: price, fit, color, fashion, style, appearance, quality of construction, durability, comfort, and care. Which factors are most important for this item and its end use? Which are least important? What are the rankings of the other factors?

With the end use and a realization of the factors that are important for serviceability of the item in mind, a possible sequence of steps in making the decision might include:

1. Determine a price range or price ceiling for the textile product.

2. Find items that are acceptable by checking available sources, such as local stores and catalogs.

3. Evaluate color, fashion, style, appearance, and quality of construction.

4. Evaluate the serviceability of the textile components of the item.

5. Buy a specific item or decide to do more shopping.

The satisfaction that the consumer receives from the textile material will depend on individual values as well as on the performance of the product. The performance and care of the product depend on the fibers, yarns, fabric construction, and finishes. The manufacturer has decided what combination would be appropriate for the item. The buyer has determined the selection available to the consumer. The final step in the decision-making process is for the consumer to select the item that is most appropriate for his or her own use.

This seems like an involved procedure to follow when shopping for an item, but most of the steps are almost automatic. The choice of where to shop limits the selection. Once in the store, price, fit, color, fashion, style, appearance, and quality of construction can be quickly evaluated. When the selection is narrowed down to two or three items, the consumer can evaluate the serviceability of the textile components of each item. This is where a student of textiles will have more knowledge than a typical customer and will be better able to match end-use requirements to a realistic expected performance of the item.

The serviceability concepts that are used in organizing the material in this book are simple and straightforward. These concepts provide a framework for combining textile facts with personal needs and preferences in a way that will help consumers make wiser decisions about the textile products they purchase and use. As the concepts are combined with the consumer's past and present experiences, they can act as a simple checklist while the purchasing decision is made. The serviceability concepts also provide an excellent framework for the pre-selector. Combined with their experience of what sells and what works for their clients, the serviceability concepts can improve their purchasing decisions.

The *five serviceability concepts* will be used by following through with the examples discussed earlier in this chapter.

1. *Aesthetics*. The bedspread for the model home should be attractive in and of itself; it must also coordinate very well with the décor of the master bedroom and blend well with the overall effect intended for the entire house. The teenager's slacks will need to look good as judged by the individual and his or her peers.

2. *Durability*. The coat for the nine-year-old should be durable enough to withstand hard use. Is it intended to be a summer, fall, spring, or winter jacket? How different are the seasons in that specific location? How quickly is the child growing—does the child tend to wear out clothes or out-grow them? Is the jacket expected to last a season, a year, or several years? The bedspread for college use will be expected to last several years and will be subjected to hard use since dorm beds usually function as sofas.

3. *Comfort*. This factor may be of great importance for a summer suit worn primarily out-of-doors in a hot and humid climate. Comfort also is very important for the person in the nursing home. The fabric must be comfortable next to delicate skin.

4. *Appearance retention*. The suit that will be worn at work needs to resist wrinkles during wear. It should maintain its shape during use. Over the period of time it is worn, it should continue to look professional. The sheets and bedspread for college use will undoubtedly last several years, but how will they look the last year?

5. *Care*. The college student's coat may not need cleaning often. If dry cleaning is required, the coat may be acceptable if it is infrequent. On the other hand, the child's jacket and the teenager's slacks probably should be washable. Slacks used in a nursing home will need to withstand high-

temperature washing and will look better after care if made from a wrinkle-resistant fabric.

When selecting among several possibly acceptable items for a specific end use, the serviceability concepts can be posed as questions. See the table, "Serviceability Questions."

To further emphasize the importance of defining the end use for a textile item and to better understand the impact this has on selection, the five serviceability concepts for each suit discussed above have been ranked by a consumer. The most important concept is ranked "1," least important concept is ranked "5." Another consumer might rank these concepts differently

Serviceability Questions

Aesthetics	Is this item attractive and appropriate in appearance for its end use? How does it look and feel?
Durability	Will this item continue to be useable for as long as expected? Or will it wear out sooner than desired?
Comfort	Is this item comfortable enough for use in its purpose? Will it be too warm or too cool? Will it feel good against the skin? Will the comfort change as the fabric wears? Will the comfort be altered by required care procedures?
Appearance retention	Will this item retain its appearance during use and care? Will it resist wrinkles? Will it retain its shape? Do the aspects that make this item attractive have suitable durability, comfort, and care characteristics? Will the item look and feel good as long as it lasts?
Care	Are the treatments required to maintain the new look of this item during use, cleaning, and storage acceptable considering the money and time available? Is the care realistic considering the cost of the item?
Serviceability	What combination of these five concepts is important in making this item useable for its purpose?

Suit

End Use	Casual: Summer	Work: Fall, Winter, and Spring
Aesthetics	3	1
Durability	5	4
Comfort	1	3
Appearance retention	4	2
Care	2	5

and some concepts may be ranked equally important.

It is most unlikely that a single textile product would be serviceable for both end uses. The needs for each end use are different. Also, another consumer might have ranked the concepts in a different order.

Finally, more than one factor will need to be considered in each end use. Let us look at the suit for work. Aesthetics factors might include a fashion look appropriate for that particular job and company of a color and style becoming to the wearer. Durability requirements would specify how long the suit is expected to be worn—one, two, or more years? Comfort factors include some minimum level of comfort because it is difficult to concentrate if clothes are scratchy or otherwise uncomfortable. Appearance-retention factors might relate to wrinkle resistance. The suit should retain its shape. It should continue to look professional for a reasonable time. Care factors include the method required. Frequently, dry cleaning is required for suits. Care was ranked of lowest priority, so presumably any care method is acceptable.

Now, to return to the shopping process—once several acceptable items have been identified, evaluate the serviceability concepts of aesthetics, durability, comfort, appearance retention, and care. Which item best satisfies the requirements of the end use? Is the cost appropriate?

Are all the other selection factors acceptable? Based on this evaluation, make the decision to purchase a specific item.

In summary, end use determines performance requirements. During selection, relate end-use performance requirements to realistic expected performance in the five serviceability areas. Within this framework, textile knowledge can be critical in satisfying needs and wants. The serviceability concepts are defined and discussed in detail in the previous chapter. The concepts are referred to frequently throughout the remainder of the book.

It must be stressed that neither this book nor any course in textiles will give students the answers for any end use. This book will not answer the question: What is the best combination of fiber, yarn, fabrication, and finish for a coat or chair? Consumers make choices based on knowledge of themselves, their needs and expectations, and the use the product will get. If they know about textiles, they can make an intelligent selection. However, with any selection, there will be some good and some not-so-good features. The more knowledge consumers have, the more serviceable the product should be.

Consumers have information available to them on labels, hang tags, and packages. Federal legislation requires that fiber content be stated. With the information in this book, fiber-content information will provide some basis for predicting performance related to durability, comfort, and appearance retention. Aesthetics can be judged by the consumer. Care labels are required by federal legislation. Thus some information is available on which to base rational decisions. How wisely that information is used, or how meaningful that information is to any one person, depends on the person making the choices. In addition, evaluation of other aspects of the product, such as yarn and fabric type, will provide more information on which to base a decision.

4
Cotton

Cotton is the most important apparel fiber throughout the world. A study done by the International Cotton Advisory Committee showed that, in developing countries with a high average temperature, cotton holds 75 percent of the market for apparel. Blends with polyester also are used, but the demand for synthetic fibers is low. On the other hand, in developed countries with a low average temperature, cotton accounts for about 30 percent of the fiber used. In the United States, in 1985, cotton accounted for more than 34 percent of fibers used in apparel.

Cotton has a combination of properties—pleasing appearance, comfort, easy washability, moderate cost, and durability—that make it ideal for warm-weather clothing, active sportswear, work clothes, towels, and sheets. This unique combination of properties has made cotton a standard for people who live in warm and subtropical climates. Even though the manmade fibers have encroached on the markets that were once dominated by 100 percent cotton fabrics, the cotton-look is still maintained, and cotton forms an important part of blended fabrics.

Cotton cloth was used by the people of ancient China, Egypt, India, Mexico, and Peru. Fabrics of cloth from Egypt give some evidence that cotton may have been used there in 12,000 B.C., before flax was known. Cotton spinning and weaving as an industry began in India, and fabrics of good-quality cotton cloth were being produced as early as 1500 B.C. The Pima Indians were growing cotton when the Spaniards came to the New World. One of the items that Columbus took back to Queen Isabella was a hank of cotton yarn.

Cotton was grown in the Southern colonies as soon as they were established. Cotton was planted in Florida in 1556 and in Virginia in the early 1600s. Records show cotton seeds imported from Egypt were planted in Jamestown, Virginia, in 1617. England encouraged cotton production in the colonies and imported the bulk of cotton produced. Throughout the 1600s and 1700s, cotton fibers had to be separated from the cotton seeds by hand. This was a very time-consuming and tedious job; a worker could separate the seeds from the fibers of only one pound of cotton in a day.

With the invention of the saw-tooth cotton gin by Eli Whitney in 1793, the scene began to change. The gin could process 50 pounds of cotton in a day; thus more cotton could be prepared for spinning. Within the next 20 years, a series of spinning and weaving inventions in England mechanized fabric production. The Industrial Revolution was underway! The British cotton-textile trade grew tremendously from 1800–1850.

The other critical factor at this time was the supply of raw cotton. The Southern states were able to meet the greatly increased demand in Britain for raw cotton. The soil and climate of the Southern states were ideal for growing cotton. Small- and medium-sized farms continued to be important, but plantations with large fields and slave labor flourished.

In 1792, 6,000 bales of cotton were produced by the Southern states. Seven years later, with the introduction of the cotton gin, production reached 100,000 bales. The United States was the most important supplier of cotton to the British textile industry for the next 60 years. By 1859, U.S. production was 4.5 million bales of cotton—⅔ of the world production. Cotton was the leading U.S. export.

The picture again changed dramatically with the U.S. Civil War. U.S. cotton production decreased to 200,000 bales in 1864, and Britain looked to other countries to fill her needs. After the war, Western states began producing cotton.

During the time of rapidly expanding cotton production in the Southern states, the New England states were building factories to manufacture yarn and fabric. In 1790, Samuel Slater built the first yarn-spinning mill in Pawtucket, Rhode Island. For the next 150 years, most spinning and weaving of U.S. fabrics took place in the New England states.

After the Civil War, the Southern states began building spinning and weaving mills. Between World War I and World War II, most of the New England mills moved south. Factors important in this change of location included being closer to the supply of cotton, having cheaper power, using less-expensive nonunion labor, and receiving special incentives from state and local governments to encourage companies to set up a mill in their town and state. By 1950, 80 percent of the mills were in the South. In the 1980s, many mills have closed because of increased costs and competition from imported fabrics.

PRODUCTION

Cotton grows in any part of the world where the growing season is long and the climate is temperate to hot with adequate rainfall or irrigation. Cellulose will not form if the temperature is below 70°F. In the United States, cotton is grown from southern South Carolina west to central California and south of that line. Figure 4–1 shows where cotton is currently produced in the United States. Much of the cotton produced in the U.S. is exported.

Upland cotton is the most important kind of cotton grown in the United States. In 1985, 13.7 million bales were produced, with an estimated 5.75 million bales being used by U.S. mills. The rest were exported. Extra-long staple cotton is grown in Arizona, Texas, and New Mexico. The United States produced 148,000 bales of American Pima cotton in 1985 and much of this long-staple cotton was exported.

The United States was the top producer of cotton through 1977. The Soviet Union was the top producer in 1978 and 1980, with the United States leading in 1979 and again in 1981. China took the lead in 1982 and continues to lead in production through 1986.

Factors affecting the U.S. production of cotton include the increasing value of the U.S. dollar compared with other currencies, the increasing imports of cotton apparel and fabrics, the changes in government incentives for growing cotton, and the changes in other countries. One of the most important changes is the emergence of China in world trade with its increased exports and production of cotton and other fibers.

In 1985, world production of cotton was 80.9 million bales. The People's Republic of China produced 28.5 percent of that total; the United States 16.9 percent; and the Soviet Union 15.5

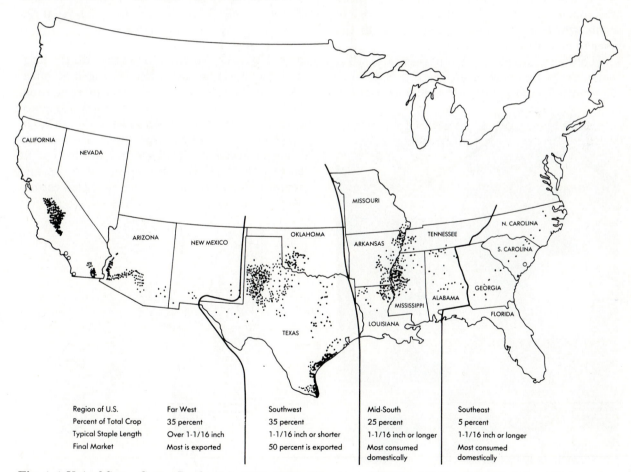

Region of U.S.	Far West	Southwest	Mid-South	Southeast
Percent of Total Crop	35 percent	35 percent	25 percent	5 percent
Typical Staple Length	Over 1-1/16 inch	1-1/16 inch or shorter	1-1/16 inch or longer	1-1/16 inch or longer
Final Market	Most is exported	50 percent is exported	Most consumed domestically	Most consumed domestically

Fig. 4–1 *United States Cotton Production, 1984–1985. (Courtesy of National Cotton Council of America.)*

percent. India, fourth in production, consistently produces 8–9 percent of the world's production. In 1985, Pakistan, Brazil, Turkey, and Egypt produced over one million bales each, which is 2–4 percent of the world's production.

Cotton grows on bushes 3–6 feet high. The blossom appears, falls off, and the *boll* begins its growth. Inside the boll are seeds from which the fibers grow. When the boll is ripe, it splits open, and the fluffy white fibers stand out like a powder puff (a boll contains seven or eight seeds) (Figure 4–2). Each cotton seed may have as many as 20,000 fibers growing from its surface.

Cotton is picked by machine or by hand (Figure 4–3). Machine-picked cotton contains many immature fibers—an inescapable result of stripping a cotton plant. However, mechanization and weed control have reduced the number of hours required to produce a bale of cotton. After picking, the cotton is taken to a *gin* to remove the fibers from the seed. Figure 4–4 shows a saw gin, in which the whirling saws pick up the fiber and carry it to a knife-like comb, which blocks the seeds and permits the fiber to be carried through.

The fibers, called *lint*, are pressed into bales weighing 480 pounds, ready for sale to a spinning mill. The average yield is 629 pounds per

Fig. 4–3 Cotton field with harvester. (Courtesy of National Cotton Council of America.)

acre. However, Arizona, the state with the largest production per acre, has averaged as much as 863 pounds per acre. The seeds, after ginning, look like the buds of the pussywillow. They are covered with very short fibers—⅛ inch in length—called *linters*. The linters are removed from the seeds and are used to a limited extent as raw material for the making of rayon and acetate. The seeds are crushed to obtain cottonseed oil and meal.

Fig. 4–2 Opened cotton boll. (Courtesy of National Cotton Council of America.)

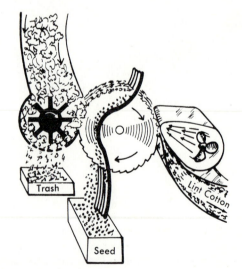

Fig. 4–4 Cotton gin.

Fiber Properties

PHYSICAL STRUCTURE

Raw cotton is creamy white in color. The fiber is a single cell, which grows out of the seed as a hollow cylindrical tube over one thousand times as long as it is thick.

The *quality* of cotton depends on its length, strength, fineness, and maturity. Other factors affecting quality are color, leaf residue, and ginning preparation.

Length. Staple length is very important because it affects how the fiber is handled during spinning and it relates to fiber fineness and fiber tensile strength. Longer cotton fibers are finer and make stronger yarns.

Cotton fibers range in length from ½ inch to 2 inches, depending on the variety. There are three groups of cotton that are commercially important:

1. Upland cottons, which are ⅞–1¼ inches in length and were developed from cottons native to Mexico and Central America.

2. Long staple cottons, which are 1⁵⁄₁₆–1½ inches in length and were developed from Egyptian and South American cottons. Different varieties include American Pima, Egyptian, American Egyptian, and Sea Island cottons.

3. Short staple cottons, which are less than ¾ inch in length and are produced primarily in India and eastern Asia.

Long staple fibers are considered to be finer quality because they can be made into softer, smoother, stronger, and more-lustrous fabrics. Because they command a higher price and less is produced than the medium- and short-staple lengths, they are sometimes identified on a label or tag as Pima or Supima. Or they may be referred to as long-staple or extra-long-staple cotton.

Convolutions. *Convolutions,* or ribbon-like twists, characterize the cotton fibers (Figure 4–5). When the fibers mature, the boll opens, the fibers dry out, and the central canal collapses; reverse spirals cause the fibers to twist. The twist forms a natural crimp that enables the fi-

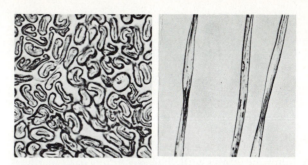

Fig. 4–5 *Photomicrographs of cotton: cross-sectional view at 500× (left); longitudinal view 250× (right). (Courtesy of E. I. du Pont de Nemours & Company.)*

bers to cohere to one another, so that despite its short length, cotton is one of the most spinnable fibers. The convolutions can be a disadvantage, since dirt collects in the twists and must be removed by vigorous washing. Long-staple cotton has about 300 convolutions per inch; short-staple cotton has less than 200.

Fineness. Cotton fibers vary from 16–20 micrometers in diameter. The cross-sectional shape varies with the maturity of the fiber. Immature fibers tend to be U-shaped and the cell wall is thinner; mature fibers are more nearly circular, with a very small central canal. In every cotton boll there are immature fibers. The proportion of immature to mature fibers cause problems in processing, especially in spinning and dyeing. Notice in the photomicrograph of the cross-section the difference in size and shape.

Distinctive Parts. The cotton fiber is made up of a cuticle, primary wall, secondary wall, and lumen (Figure 4–6). The fiber grows to almost full length as a hollow tube before the secondary wall begins to form.

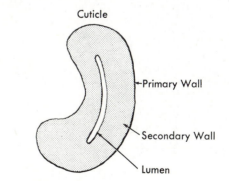

Cuticle

Primary Wall

Secondary Wall

Lumen

Fig. 4–6 *Cross-section of mature cotton fiber.*

Fig. 4—7 Layers of cellulose (schematic).

The *cuticle* is a wax-like film covering the primary, or outer, wall. The *secondary wall* is made up of layers of cellulose (Figure 4–7).

The layers deposited at night differ in density from those deposited during the day; this causes *growth rings,* which can be seen in the cross-section. The cellulose layers are composed of *fibrils*—bundles of cellulose chains—arranged spirally. At some points the fibrils reverse direction. These *reverse spirals* (Figure 4–8) are an important factor in the convolutions, elastic recovery, and elongation of the fiber. They are also the weak spots, being 15–30 percent weaker than the rest.

Cellulose is deposited daily for 20–30 days until, in the mature fiber, the fiber tube is almost filled.

The *lumen* is the central canal, through which the nourishment travels during growth. When the fiber matures, the dried nutrients in the lumen give the characteristic dark areas that can be seen with the microscope.

Color. Cotton is naturally creamy white. As it ages, it becomes more beige. If it is rained on just before harvest, the fiber is grayer. White fiber is preferred.

Picking and ginning affect the appearance of cotton fibers. Carefully picked cotton is cleaner. Well-ginned cotton is uniform in appearance

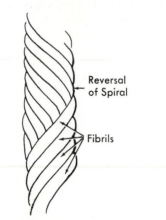

Reversal of Spiral

Fibrils

Fig. 4–8 Reverse spirals in cotton fiber.

and white in color. Poorly ginned cotton will have brown flecks in it, called *trash,* such as bits of leaf or stem or dirt. These brown flecks decrease the quality of the fiber. Fabrics made from such fibers are suitable for utility cloths and occasionally are fashionable when a "natural" look is popular.

Grading and classing of cotton is done by hand and by machine. Visual inspection of staple length and color compare the cotton from the bale being graded with standards prepared by the United States Department of Agriculture.

COTTON CLASSIFICATION

Cotton classification is the art of describing quality of cotton in terms of grade and staple length. *Staple length* is identified by using sight and touch and experience to determine the length of a representative bundle of fibers from a bale of cotton. A good cotton classer must be able to tell consistently differences in length of $\frac{1}{32}$ of an inch. Actually, a sample classified as $1\frac{5}{32}$ inch will have fibers ranging in length from $\frac{1}{8}$ inch to $1\frac{5}{8}$ inch as shown in Figure 4–9.

The grade of cotton is determined by its appearance—more specifically, by its color, leaf residue, and preparation. There are 40 grades for upland cotton. The predominant grade of cotton produced in the United States is strict low-middling cotton. *Strict* in this case means "better than."

Color of cotton is described in terms that range from white to yellow: white, light-spotted, spotted, tinged, and yellow. Color is also described in terms of lightness to darkness: plus, light gray, and gray. This factor of appearance is a combination of grayness and the amount of leaf present in white-cotton grades.

Grading of American Egyptian cotton is based on ten grades. It is yellower in appearance than upland cotton and has a different appearance after ginning because it is done on a different kind of gin and has a higher leaf content.

Cotton is a commodity crop. It is sold by grade and staple length. Strict low-middling cotton is used in mass-produced cotton goods and in cotton/synthetic blends. Better grades of cotton and longer-staple cotton are used in quality shirtings and sheets. Extra-long-staple American Egyptian cotton is frequently identified by the terms Pima and Supima because of its higher

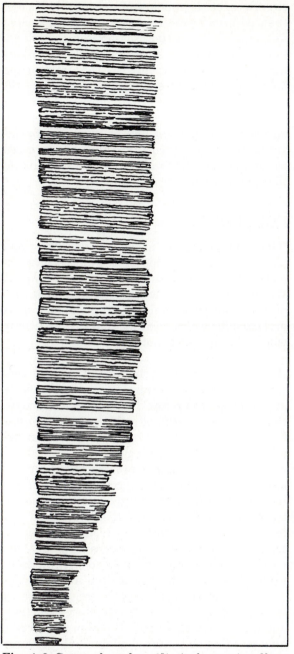

Fig. 4–9 *Cotton classed as 1⁵/₃₂ inch contains fibers that range in length from less than ⅛ inch up to 1⁵/₈ inch. (Courtesy of United States Department of Agriculture.)*

quality and price. Pima is seen in women's sweaters, women's panties, and towels.

CHEMICAL COMPOSITION AND MOLECULAR ARRANGEMENT

Cotton, when picked, is about 94 percent cellulose; in finished fabrics it is 99 percent cellulose.

Like all cellulose fibers, cotton contains carbon, hydrogen, and oxygen with reactive hydroxyl (OH) groups. Cotton may have as many as 10,000 glucose residues per molecule. The molecular chains are in spiral form.

The basic unit of the cellulose molecule is the *glucose unit*. The glucose unit is made up of the chemical elements carbon, hydrogen, and oxygen.

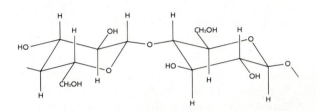

CHEMICAL NATURE OF CELLULOSE

The chemical reactivity of cellulose is related to the three hydroxyl groups (OH groups) of the glucose unit. These groups react readily with moisture, dyes, and many finishes. Chemicals such as bleaches cause a breakdown of the molecular chain of the cellulose, usually by attacking the oxygen atom and causing a rupture there.

The cellulose molecule is a long, linear chain of glucose units. The length of the chain is a factor in fiber strength.

Mercerization. John Mercer, using a cotton cloth to filter a caustic soda (or sodium hydroxide, NaOH) solution, noticed that the cloth was changed during the process. He demonstrated the beneficial effects of caustic soda on cotton and from that time (1844) on, *mercerization* of cotton has been a common finish for yarns and fabrics (see Chapter 32). Mercerization (treating yarns or fabrics with NaOH) causes a physical change in the fiber. In *tension mercerization,* the fabric or yarn being mercerized is under tension. The concentration of the sodium hydroxide solution is high, generally around 20 percent. The sodium hydroxide causes the fiber to swell. Because of the tension during the swelling, the fibers become more rod-like and rounder in cross-section, and the number of convolutions decreases (Figure 4–10).

The following are effects of tension mercerization:

- *Increased strength* to the fibers. The molecular chains are less-spiral in form and are more-oriented in length, making the fibers 30 percent stronger.

- *Increased absorbency* because the fiber swells. This opens up the molecular structure so that more moisture can be absorbed. The moisture regain is 11 percent. Mercerization is done primarily to improve the dyeability of cotton yarns and fabrics.

- *Increased luster* because the fibers become rounder with fewer convolutions and thus reflect more light. Mercerization for luster is done under tension and on long-staple cotton yarns and fabrics.

A second type of mercerization is often referred to as *slack mercerization* because no tension is used. In this process, the fabric or yarn is soaked in a weaker solution of sodium hydroxide than the solution used in tension mercerization. Slack mercerization is done primarily to increase the absorbency and to improve the dyeability of cotton yarns and fabrics.

Liquid Ammonia Finishes. Liquid ammonia is used as an alternative to several preparation finishes, especially mercerization. Liquid ammonia is used on cellulosic-fiber contents and blends with cellulosics. The ammonia swells the fiber, but not to the degree of sodium hydroxide. Fabrics that have had the ammonia treatment have good luster and dyeability. These fabrics do not dye to the same depth as mercerized fabrics. Because the amount of resin needed is less than with mercerized fabrics, ammonia-treated fabrics will have better crease recovery and less loss of strength and abrasion resistance following wrinkle-resistant finishes than mercerized fabrics. Ammonia-treated fabrics are less stiff and harsh than mercerized fabrics. Ammonia treated fabrics have an increase in tensile strength of 40 percent and an increase in elongation of two to three times that of untreated cotton. These fabrics also are less sensitive to thermal degradation.

PROPERTIES

"Once you get a feel for cotton, you won't feel like anything else." This phrase was used to promote cotton in *American Fabrics and Fashions*, Winter 1982. Cotton is a comfortable fiber. Appropriate for year-round use, it is the fiber most preferred for warm-weather clothing, especially where the climate is hot and humid.

Aesthetic. Cotton fabrics certainly have consumer acceptance. Cotton fabrics have a matte appearance. Their low luster is the standard that has been retained with cotton/polyester blends that are increasingly important in apparel and home-furnishing fabrics.

Cotton fabrics with more luster than usual are available. Long-staple cottons make more-lustrous fabrics. Mercerized and ammonia-treated cotton fabrics have a soft, pleasant luster as a result of chemical finishes. Cotton sateen has a luster due to weave structure and possible finishes. Cotton blended with lustrous rayon results in a lustrous cotton-like fabric.

Drape, texture, and hand are affected by choice of yarn size and type, fabric structure, and finish. Soft, sheer batiste; crisp, sheer voile; fine percale; and sturdy denim and corduroy have been popular for years.

Durability. Cotton is a medium strength fiber having a breaking tenacity of 3.5–4.0 g/d. It is stronger when wet. Long-staple cotton makes stronger yarns because there are more points of contact between the fibers when they are twisted together. Because of its higher wet strength, cotton can stand rough handling during laundering.

Abrasion resistance is moderate. Obviously, heavy denim fabrics or corduroy will take longer

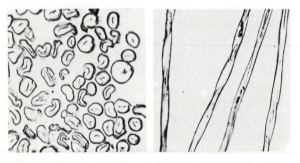

Fig. 4–10 *Photomicrographs of mercerized cotton: cross-sectional view 500× (left); longitudinal view 250× (right). (Courtesy of E. I. du Pont de Nemours & Company.)*

Summary of the Performance of Cotton in Apparel Fabrics

AESTHETIC	ATTRACTIVE
Luster	Matte, pleasant
Drape	Soft to stiff
Texture	Pleasant
Hand	Smooth to rough
DURABILITY	MODERATE
Abrasion resistance	Moderate
Tenacity	Moderate
Elongation	Low
COMFORT	EXCELLENT
Absorbancy	Excellent
Thermal retention	Low
APPEARANCE RETENTION	MODERATE
Resiliency	Low
Dimensional stability	Moderate
Elastic recovery	Moderate
RECOMMENDED CARE	MACHINE WASH AND DRY

to wear through than thinner shirting fabrics. The *elongation* of cotton is low, 3 percent, and it has low elasticity.

Comfort. Cotton makes very comfortable skin-contact fabrics because of its high absorbency and its good heat and electrical conductivity. It is lacking in any surface characteristics that might be irritating to the skin. Cotton has a moisture regain of 7 percent. When cotton becomes wet, the fibers swell and become somewhat plastic. This property makes it possible to give a smooth, flat finish to cotton fabrics when they are ironed, and makes high-count woven fabrics water repellent. However, as cotton fabrics absorb more moisture, they feel wet or clammy—think of dish or bath towels.

Cotton is a comfortable fiber to wear in hot and humid weather. The fibers absorb moisture and feel good against the skin in high humidity. The fiber ends in the spun yarn hold the fabric slightly off the skin for greater comfort. Moisture passes freely through the fabric, thus aiding evaporation and cooling. Cotton is very comfortable for wear all year—heavier fabrics such as denim and corduroy are usually cotton and are perennial favorites for fall and winter wear

in some areas. However, in cold rain or snow, cotton may be too absorbent to be comfortable.

Appearance Retention. Overall appearance retention is moderate. Cotton has very low resiliency. The hydrogen bonds holding the molecular chains together are weak, and when fabrics are bent or crushed, particularly in the presence of moisture, the chains move freely to new positions. When pressure is removed, there are no forces within the fibers to pull the chains back to their original positions so the fabrics stay wrinkled. Creases can be ironed in easily, and wrinkles can be pressed out easily, but wrinkling while wearing remains a problem.

Unless cotton fabrics are given a durable-press finish, or blended with polyester and given a durable-press finish, they wrinkle easily during both wear and care. The wrinkled look is very popular at times—wrinkles are even added during finishing so they will remain. However, at other times, fashion dictates a neat, nonwrinkled look.

All-cotton denim and all-cotton knits will shrink unless they have been given a durable-press finish or a shrinkage-resistant finish. Untreated cottons shrink less when washed in cool water and drip dried; they shrink more when washed in hot water and dried in a hot drier. When they are worn again, they tend to recover some of their original dimensions—think of your experiences with cotton-denim jeans.

All-cotton fabrics and garments that have been given a wrinkle-resistant or durable-press finish or have been treated for shrinkage generally should not shrink noticeably. However, you may need to be a little more careful of hand-woven cotton fabrics or those imported from India and China, unless specific information about shrinkage is available on the label.

Elastic recovery is moderate. Cotton recovers 75 percent from 2–5 percent stretch. In other words, cotton tends to stay stretched out in areas of stress, such as in the elbow or knee areas of garments.

Care. Cotton requires no special care during washing and drying. White cottons can be washed in hot water. Colored cottons will retain their color better if washed in warm water instead of hot water. If the garments are not heavily soiled, cold water will clean them adequately. Cotton releases all types of soil readily.

Chlorine bleach may be used on cottons if the directions are followed; bleaching should be considered a spot-removal method and not be routinely used with every load of wash. Excessive bleaching weakens cellulosic fibers.

Less wrinkling will occur in the dryer if the cotton garments are removed when they are dry and not left in the dryer longer than necessary. Ironing is not as common at present. For many cotton clothes, a steam iron is adequate to remove wrinkles. However, some all-cotton clothes respond better to pressing while damp with a hot and dry iron. These cottons will iron nicely, but they handle differently than blends do. Polyester/cotton fabrics need to be ironed at a lower temperature to avoid melting the polyester.

Cottons should be stored clean and dry. If they are damp, mildew can form. Mildew first appears as little black dots, but it can actually eat through the fabric, causing holes if enough time elapses. If the clothing merely smells of mildew, it can be laundered or bleached and it will be fine. But if the mildew has progressed to visible spots, they may or may not be removable. More-extensive damage cannot be corrected.

Cotton is harmed by acids. Fruit and fruit-juice stains should be promptly treated with cold water before they set and become even more difficult to remove. Cotton is not greatly harmed by alkalis. Cotton can be washed with strong detergents and under proper conditions it will withstand chlorine bleaches. Cotton is resistant to organic solvents so that it can be safely dry-cleaned.

Cotton oxidizes in sunlight, which causes white and pastel cottons to yellow and all cotton to degrade. Some dyes are especially sensitive to sunlight and when used in window-treatment fabrics the dyed areas disintegrate.

Cotton is not thermoplastic. It can safely be ironed at high temperatures. Cotton burns readily.

USES

Cotton is the most important apparel fiber in the United States. In 1983, it accounted for 37.5 percent of apparel fabrics. (Polyester was a close second with 35 percent of apparel fabrics.) Cotton had been the most widely used fiber for apparel, home furnishing, and industrial uses for over 125 years, but in 1973, 1974, and 1975, both cotton and polyester were used almost equally. By 1976, polyester was used more widely than cotton when all uses were combined.

A report in *The Cotton Situation*, November 1985, by the United States Department of Agriculture, stated:

Years from now, the U.S. textile industry may look back on 1985/86 as the season when cotton finally turned the corner, once and for all, in its competition with man-made fibers. "Natural" blend pants and shirts of 60 percent cotton and 40 percent polyester are increasingly available at retail stores. Use of heavyweight, 100-percent denim is rising, and the cotton content of other apparel products, ranging from socks and underwear to women's wear, is increasing.

A shift in consumer preferences toward natural fibers, improved technology for using cotton, a fashion trend toward heavyweight denim, and a decline in the cotton/polyester price ratio, combined with a perception that cotton will remain relatively less expensive, underlie the rise in cotton's market share. The influence of trends in fashion and consumer preferences cannot be quantified, but cotton's share of domestic consumption began rising in 1980. . . . Retailers indicate that shifts in consumer tastes are causing these changes." (pp. 4–5)

Other people closely associated with cotton agree that cotton's share of the market is rising, but they think discussing competition between fibers is an outdated approach. Blends are too important a part of the market to be ignored. The increased usage of cotton will come from (1) greater use of 100 percent cotton in apparel; (2) increased availability of cotton-rich blends (those with 60 percent or more cotton) in apparel; and (3) more cotton used with other fibers to replace 100 percent man-made fiber fabrics, especially in bottom-weight fabrics.

Looking at cotton as a part of the total fiber market, cotton accounts for the following percentages of fiber used in these broad end-use categories in 1985:

· 40 percent of apparel
· 19 percent of home furnishings
· 16 percent of industrial uses

Major End Uses of Cotton—1985

Percent of Cotton's Share of Market		Thousand Bales*	Percent of Market Share Held by Cotton
40%	*APPAREL*		
	Men's and boys' trousers and shorts	854	67%
	Men's and boys' shirts	558	53
	Men's and boys' underwear	373	71
	Women's and misses slacks and jeans	369	51
	Women's and misses blouses and shirts	163	32
	Women's and misses dresses	83	20
	Men's and boys' gloves and mittens	82	84
	Men's and boys linings and pockets	79	23
	Girls' and children's slacks and jeans	67	55
	Girls' and children's hosiery	57	39
	Girls' and children's blouses and shirts	50	44
	Men's hosiery	49	22
19%	*HOME FURNISHINGS*		
	Towels and wash cloths	685	93%
	Sheets and pillowcases	406	48
	Drapes, upholstery, and slipcovers	387	28
	Bedspreads	90	44
	Tablecloths, napkins, and placements	50	52
	Rugs and carpets	38	1
	Comforters and quilts	29	43
	Blankets	27	14
	Curtains	27	14
16%	*INDUSTRIAL AND OTHER CONSUMER PRODUCTS*		
	Medical supplies	143	52%
	Retail piece goods	138	33
	Thread, industrial	88	30
	Tarpaulins	70	54
	Abrasives	54	87
27	Overall market share		

*480-lb bales.
Source: Cotton Counts Its Customers, 1986, National Cotton Council.

Focusing on cotton alone, of the 2,980 million pounds of cotton consumed in the United States in 1984, the following percentages were used:

· 57 percent of cotton went into apparel
· 27 percent of cotton went into home furnishings
· 13 percent of cotton went into industrial uses
· 3 percent of cotton went into exports

Details of specific end uses within those broad categories are given in the table, "Major End Uses of Cotton—1985."

The greatest amount of cotton is used for apparel. All-cotton fabrics are used where comfort is of primary importance and appearance retention is not as important—or where a more-casual plissé fabric or crinkle cotton is acceptable. Cotton blended with polyester in durable-press fabrics is much easier to find on the market, both in ready-to-wear apparel and in over-the-counter fabrics. It is possible to find cotton-rich blends if you look for them—60 percent or 70 percent cotton blended with polyester and given a durable-press finish. Most blends retain the pleasant appearance of cotton, have the same or increased durability, are less comfortable in conditions of extreme heat and humidity or high physical activity, and have better appearance retention during wear in comparison with 100 percent cotton fabrics. However, removal of oily soil is a greater problem with blends.

The statistics on end use do not distinguish between all-cotton items and cotton blends. What is in your wardrobe? What blend levels are present? Do you have all-cotton garments? Do you prefer all cotton for some uses? The last column in the table, "Major End Uses of Cotton—1985," gives some indication of how important cotton and cotton blends are in the specific end uses.

Cotton, Inc., is the organization that promotes the use of cotton by consumers. This organization wants people to recognize the seal of cotton trademark. They also have been promoting the use of Natural Blend® fabrics and apparel— items that have at least 60 percent cotton in them.

Imports of cotton textiles have increased over recent years until in 1984 they totaled 3.1 million bales, or 37 percent, of domestic cotton consumption. Half of the imports are cotton apparel, 30 percent of imports are cotton fabrics— Hong Kong is the largest supplier. Korea, Taiwan, and China are all important suppliers. What have your experiences been with the performance of these imported garments? Can you make generalized comparisons about the quality or performance differences, if any, between garments imported from different countries?

Cotton is also a very important home-furnishing fabric. Towels are mostly cotton—softness, absorbency, wide range of colors, and washability are important in this end use. Durability is increased in the base fabric, as well as in the selvages and hems by blending polyester with the cotton. However, the loops of the towel are all cotton so that maximum absorbency is retained.

Sheets and pillowcases are mostly blends of cotton with polyester. All-cotton sheets are

Fig. 4–11 *Cotton® seal* (top) *for fabrics and apparel made of 100 percent cotton and Natural Blend® seal* (bottom) *for fabrics and apparel made of at least 60 percent cotton.*

available. Blend levels and counts vary a great deal. Muslin and percale sheets are common, and flannelette sheets are available in the fall and winter. Spring- and fall-weight blankets made of cotton are also on the market. Cotton bedspreads are available in a variety of weights.

Drapes, curtains, upholstery fabrics, and slipcovers are made of cotton, as well as of polyester/cotton blends. Many heavyweight cotton upholstery fabrics are very attractive and very durable. They are comfortable and easy to spot clean. They retain their appearance well. Resiliency is not a problem with heavyweight fabrics that are stretched over the furniture frame.

Medical supplies are frequently cotton. Since cotton can be autoclaved (heated to a high temperature to sanitize it), it is very important in hospitals. Absorbency, washability, and low static build-up are also important properties in hospital uses.

Industrial uses include abrasives, book bindings, luggage and handbags, shoes and slippers, tobacco cloth, woven wiping cloths, and wall-covering fabrics.

5

Flax and Other Natural Cellulosic Fibers

All plants are fibrous. The fiber bundles of plants give strength and pliability to their stems, leaves, and roots. Natural cellulosic textile fibers are obtained from plants where the fibers can be readily and economically separated from the rest of the plant. They can be classified according to the portion of the plant from which they are removed (see the following chart).

Natural Cellulosic Fibers

Seed Hairs	Bast Fibers	Leaf Fibers
Cotton	Flax	Piña
Kapok	Ramie	Abaca
Coir	Hemp	Sisal
	Jute	Hennequin
	Kenaf	

Cotton, discussed in the previous chapter, is an example of a *seed fiber*. Flax is an example of a *bast fiber*, a fiber that is obtained from the stem of the plant. Sisal is an example of a *leaf fiber*.

These fibers differ in physical structure but are alike in chemical composition. The arrangement of the molecular chains in fibers, although similar, varies in orientation and length, so that performance characteristics related to polymer orientation and length will differ. Fabrics made from these fibers will thus have different appearances and hand but will react to chemicals in essentially the same way and will require essentially the same care. Properties common to all cellulosic fibers are summarized in the chart on page 37.

In this chapter, natural cellulosic fibers that account for a relatively small amount of U.S. textile fiber consumption will be discussed. Many of these fibers have found little use in the United States; nevertheless, a discussion of these fibers has a place in an introductory textiles course because some of these fibers are imported into the United States and others may be encountered during travel. Although many of these fibers are not of great importance to the U.S. economy, these fibers may be significant to the economy of the countries where they are produced. There are, of course, many other natural cellulosic fibers that will not be discussed because of their extremely limited use.

Bast Fibers

Bast fibers come from the stem of the plant. Hand labor is often required to process bast fibers, so that production of these fibers has flourished in countries where labor is cheap. Complete mechanization in the production of bast fibers has yet to be achieved. Harvesting is done by pulling or cutting the plants. Flax is usually pulled either by hand or by machine. After harvesting, the seeds are removed from the plants.

Since the fiber extends into the root, harvesting is done by pulling up the plant or cutting it close to the ground to keep fiber length as long as possible. After harvesting, the seeds are removed by pulling the plant through a machine in a process called *rippling*.

Bast fibers lie in bundles in the stem of the plant just under the outer covering or bark. They are sealed together by a substance composed of pectins, waxes, and gums. To loosen the fibers so that they can be removed from the stalk, the pectin must be decomposed by a process called *retting* (bacterial rotting). There are some individual fiber differences in the process, but the major steps are the same. Retting can be done in the fields (dew retting); in ponds or pools (pool retting); in tanks (tank retting), where the temperature and bacterial count can be carefully controlled; or in chemical retting, in which chemicals such as sodium hydroxide are used. Chemical retting is a much faster process than any other method. However, extra care must be taken or irreversible damage can occur to the fiber.

After the plants have been rinsed and dried, the woody portion is removed by breaking the outer covering, or *scutching*, in which the stalks are passed between fluted metal rollers. Most of the fibers are separated from one another, and the short fibers are removed by *hackling*, or combing. Figure 5–1 shows flax at different stages of processing.

The processes of spinning, weaving, and finishing cause further separation of the fibers. With most bast fibers, length and fineness dimensions are not clearly definable. The primary fibers are bound together in fiber bundles and never completely separate into individual fibers. These fibers, as they are commonly used, are

Properties Common to All Cellulose Fibers

Properties	Importance to Consumer
Good absorbency	Comfortable for summer wear
	Good for towels, diapers, handkerchiefs, and active sportswear
Good conductor of heat	Sheer fabrics cool for summer wear
Ability to withstand high temperature	Fabrics can be boiled or autoclaved to make relatively germ free. No special precautions in ironing
Low resiliency	Fabrics wrinkle badly unless finished for recovery
Lacks loft. Packs well into compact yarns	Tight, high-count fabrics can be made
	Makes wind-resistant fabrics
Good conductor of electricity	Does not build up static
High density (1.5±)	Fabrics are heavier than comparable fabrics of other fiber content
Harmed by mineral acids, but little affected by organic acids	Fruit stains should be removed immediately from a garment to prevent setting
Attacked by mildew	Store clean items under dry conditions
Resistant to moths, but may be damaged by crickets and silverfish	
Flammability	Cellulose fibers ignite quickly, burn freely, and have an afterglow and gray, feathery ash. Filmy or loosely constructed garments should not be worn near an open flame
Moderate resistance to sunlight	Draperies should be lined

made up of many primary fibers. It is this characteristic of fiber bundles that give bast-fiber fabrics their characteristic thick-and-thin yarns.

FLAX

Flax is one of the oldest textile fibers. Fragments of linen fabric were found in the prehistoric lake dwellings in Switzerland; linen mummy cloths, more than 3,000 years old, were found in Egyptian tombs. The linen industry flourished in Europe until the 18th century. With the invention of power spinning, cotton replaced flax as the most important and widely used fiber.

Flax is a prestige fiber as a result of its limited production and relatively high cost. The term *linen* refers to cloth made from flax. This term is, however, often misused today in referring to fabrics that look like linen—fabrics that have thick-and-thin yarns and are fairly heavy or crisp. The term *Irish linen* always refers to fabrics made from flax. (The former use of flax in sheets, tablecloths, and towels has given us the term *linens* to describe textile items—for example, bed linens and table linens.)

The unique and desirable characteristics of flax are its body, strength, and thick-and-thin fiber bundles, which give texture to fabrics. The main limitations of flax are low resiliency and lack of elasticity. Most dress and suiting linens are given wrinkle-resistant finishes.

Major producers of flax include the Soviet Union, Belgium, Ireland, and New Zealand.

Fig. 5–1 Flax fiber at different stages of processing.

Stems Before Retting | After Breaking | After Scutching | After Hackling

STRUCTURE

The primary fiber of flax averages 0.5–2.15 inches in length and a few micrometers in diameter. However, as stated earlier, these primary fibers are bound together in fiber bundles.

Flax fibers can be identified under the microscope by crosswise markings called *nodes* or *joints* (Figure 5–2). The markings on flax have been attributed to cracks or breaks during harvesting, or to irregularity in growth. The fibers may appear slightly swollen at the nodes and resemble somewhat the joints in a stalk of corn. The fibers have a small, central canal similar to the lumen in cotton. The cross-section (Figure 5–2) is several-sided, or polygonal, with rounded edges.

Flax fibers are grayish in color when dew retted, and yellowish in color when water retted. Flax has a more highly oriented molecular

Fig. 5–2 *Photomicrographs of flax: cross-sectional view* (left); *longitudinal view* (right). *(Courtesy of E. I. du Pont de Nemours & Company.)*

structure than cotton, and is, therefore, stronger than the cotton fiber.

Short flax fibers are called *tow,* and the long, combed, better-quality fibers are called *line.* Line fibers are ready for spinning into yarn. The short tow fibers must be carded to prepare them for spinning into yarns that are used in less-expensive fabrics.

CHEMICAL COMPOSITION AND MOLECULAR ARRANGEMENT

Flax is similar to cotton in its chemical composition. The major differences between the two fibers are that flax has a higher degree of poly-

Summary of the Performance of Flax in Apparel Fabrics

AESTHETICS	*EXCELLENT*
Luster	High
Texture	Thick and thin
Hand	Stiff
DURABILITY	*GOOD*
Abrasion resistance	Good
Tenacity	Good
Elongation	Low
COMFORT	*HIGH*
Absorbency	High
Thermal retention	Good
APPEARANCE RETENTION	*POOR*
Resiliency	Poor
Dimensional stability	Adequate
Elastic recovery	Low
RECOMMENDED CARE	*DRY CLEAN OR MACHINE WASH*

merization (the cellulose polymer is longer) and a greater degree of orientation and crystallinity.

PROPERTIES

Aesthetic. Flax has a high, natural luster that is broken up by the fiber bundles. The fiber bundles give an irregular appearance to yarns made from flax. This irregular appearance is part of the charm of linen fabrics. The luster of flax can be increased by pounding linen fabrics with wooden hammers, a process called *beetling*. This finish produces flat yarns with good luster. The effect is not permanent unless a resin is also used.

Because flax has a higher degree of orientation and crystallinity and the fiber diameter is larger than cotton, the resulting fabrics are stiffer in drape and harsher in hand.

Durability. Flax is strong for a natural fiber. It has a breaking tenacity of 5.5 g/d when dry and 6.5 g/d when wet. Before synthetic fibers were invented, linen thread was used to sew shoes. Flax has very low elongation of approximately 3 percent. Elasticity is poor, with a 65 percent recovery at an elongation of only 2 percent. Flax also is a stiff fiber. With poor elongation, elasticity, and stiffness, fabrics of flax should not be folded repeatedly in the same place. With repeated folding, the fabric will break. Also, avoid pressing folds when ironing linen to minimize the stress on the fibers at the fold line. Flax has good abrasion resistance for a natural fiber. The good abrasion resistance is related to the fiber's high orientation and crystallinity.

Comfort. Flax has a high moisture regain of 12 percent, and it is a good conductor of electricity. Hence, static is no problem. Flax is also a good conductor of heat, so it makes an excellent fabric for warm-weather wear. Flax has a high specific gravity of 1.54, which is the same as cotton.

Care. Flax is resistant to alkalis and organic solvents. It is also resistant to high temperatures. Linen fabrics can be dry-cleaned or washed without special care and bleached with chlorine bleaches. Linen fabrics have very low resiliency and require ironing after washing. They are more resistant to sunlight than cotton.

Crease-resistant finishes can be used on linen, but the resins usually decrease strength and abrasion resistance. The wrinkling characteristics of flax are responsible for the strong high-fashion image of linen fabrics. Linen fabrics must be stored dry, otherwise mildew will become a problem.

Uses. Flax is used primarily for fashion fabrics in both apparel and home furnishings due to its high price. Flax is common in warm-weather professional or high-fashion apparel and upholstery, table linens, and window-treatment fabrics.

Identification Tests. Flax burns readily in a manner very similar to cotton. An easy way to differentiate between these two cellulosic fibers is to study their fiber length. Cotton is seldom over 2.5 inches in length; flax is almost always longer than that. Flax is also soluble in strong acids.

RAMIE

Ramie is also known as rhea or grasscloth. It has been used for several thousand years in China. It is a tall shrub from the nettle family that requires a hot, humid climate. Ramie is a fast-growing plant that can be harvested several times a year. It has been grown in the Everglades and Gulf Coast regions of the United States, but it is not currently produced in those areas.

Ramie fibers must be separated from the plant stalk by *decortication*. In this process, the bark and woody portion of the plant stem are separated from the ramie fiber. Because this process required a lot of hand labor, ramie was not commercially important until less-labor-intensive ways of decorticating were developed. Now that relatively inexpensive ways of decorticating ramie are available, ramie is becoming a commercially important fiber. Ramie found a place in the U.S. market because it was a non-quotaed fiber in the Multi-Fiber Agreement regulating the amount of specific fibers that can be imported. For this reason, many items of ramie combined with another fiber have appeared in the United States in recent years. Ramie is produced in the People's Republic of China, the Philippines, and Brazil.

Ramie is long, lustrous, and fine. It has an absorbency similar to flax. Ramie has a density

Fig. 5–3 *Photomicrographs of ramie: cross-sectional view* (left); *longitudinal view* (right). *(Courtesy of Donna Danielson.)*

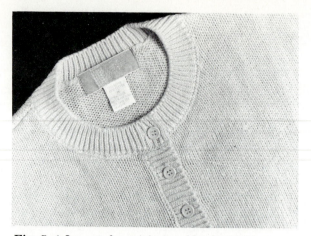

Fig. 5–4 *Imported ramie/cotton blend sweater.*

of 1.56, which is just slightly greater than that of flax.

When seen under the microscope, ramie is very similar to flax fiber (see Figure 5–3). It is pure white. It is one of the strongest fibers known and its strength increases when it is wet. It has silk-like luster. Ramie also has a very high resistance to rotting and mildew.

Ramie has some disadvantages. It is stiff and brittle, owing to the high crystallinity of its molecular structure. Consequently it lacks resiliency and is low in elasticity.

Ramie is resistant to shrinkage. It has a low elongation potential and will break if folded repeatedly in the same spot. Ramie has good absorbency, but will not dye as well as cotton. It has poor resiliency and should have a durable-press finish. Ramie is resistant to insects and microorganisms.

Ramie is used in a wide variety of imported apparel items including sweaters, shirts, blouses, and suitings (see Figure 5–4). It is often found in blends, particularly with cotton. It is also used in table linens, ropes, twines, nets, and industrial uses. Major problems experienced with ramie include its poor elasticity and color retention.

HEMP

The history of *hemp* is as old as that of flax. Hemp resembles flax; however, because hemp lacks the fineness of better-quality flax, it has never been able to compete with flax for clothing. Some varieties of hemp, though, are very difficult to distinguish from flax.

The high strength of hemp makes it particularly suitable for twine, cordage, and thread. Hemp is not very pliable or elastic. It does not rot readily when exposed to water. Hemp was commercially important up to the end of World War II. After World War II, the demand for hemp declined because many other natural and synthetic fibers took over its end uses.

JUTE

Jute was known as a fiber in Biblical times and probably was the fiber in sack cloth. Jute is one of the cheapest textile fibers, and it is second in production to cotton of all the natural cellulosic fibers. It is grown throughout Asia, chiefly in India and Bangladesh. The primary fibers in the fiber bundle are short and brittle, making jute one of the weakest of the cellulosic fibers.

Jute is creamy white to brown in color. It is soft, lustrous, and pliable when first removed from the stalk. But, on exposure to water, it turns brown, weak, and brittle. Jute has poor elasticity and elongation.

The greatest part of jute production goes into sugar and coffee bagging; it is also used for carpet backing, rope, cordage, and twine. Olefin is a strong competitor in these end uses. Because jute is losing its market, other uses for it are being investigated by jute-producing countries. For example, Bangladesh is investigating jute as a reinforcing fiber in resins to create preformed low-cost housing.

Burlap is used as a fashion fabric for decorative home furnishings. Chemical finishes can be used to overcome the natural odor and the stiffness of the fiber. Jute has low sunlight resistance and poor colorfastness. It is brittle and subject to splitting and snagging. It also deteriorates quickly when exposed to water.

KENAF

Kenaf is a soft bast fiber from the kenaf plant. The fiber is light yellow to gray, long in length, and harder and more lustrous than jute. It is used for twine, cordage, and other purposes similar to jute. Kenaf is produced in Central Asia, India, Africa, and some Central American countries. Kenaf is being investigated as a source of paper fiber.

Seed Fibers

Seed fibers are those from the seed pod of the plant. By far the most important seed fiber is cotton. In this section, some minor seed fibers will be discussed briefly.

In the production of seed fibers, the first step is separation of the fiber from the seed. With some seed fibers, the seed also is used in producing oil and feed for animals. After the seed and fiber have been separated, the fibers may be carded to get the fibers in a parallel arrangement for production of yarns or used as bundles of fibers for fiberfill.

KAPOK

Kapok is obtained from the seed of the Java kapok or silk cotton tree. The fiber is very lightweight and soft. Kapok is hollow and very buoyant. With use, kapok has a tendency to break down into a powder. The fiber is difficult to spin into yarns so it is used primarily as fiberfill for personal flotation devices and for pillow and upholstery padding.

COIR

Coir is the fiber obtained from the fibrous mass between the outer shell and the husk of the coconut. The fibers are removed by soaking the husk in saline water for several months. Coir is a very stiff, cinnamon-brown fiber. It has good abrasion, water, and weather resistance. It is used for floor mats and outdoor carpeting. Sri Lanka is the major producer of coir fiber.

Leaf Fibers

Leaf fibers are those fibers obtained from the leaf of the plant. Most leaf fibers are long and fairly stiff. In processing, the leaf is cut from the plant and the fiber is split, or pulled, from the leaf. Most of these fibers have poor dye affinity and are used in their natural color.

PIÑA

Piña is obtained from the leaves of the pineapple plant. The fiber is soft, lustrous, and white or ivory. The fiber is highly susceptible to acids and enzymes, so any acid stains should be rinsed out immediately and enzymatic presoaks should be avoided. Hand washing is recommended for piña. The fiber is used to produce lightweight sheer fabrics that are fairly stiff. These fabrics are often embroidered and used for formal wear in the Philippines. Piña is also used to make mats, bags, table linens, and clothing (see Figure 5–5).

Fig. 5–5 *Piña place mat.*

ABACA

Abaca is obtained from a member of the banana-tree family. Abaca fibers are coarse and very long; some may reach a length of 15 feet. Abaca is off-white to brown in color. The fiber is strong, durable, and flexible. It is used for ropes, cordage, floor mats, table linens, and clothing. It is produced in Central America and the Philippines. Abaca is sometimes referred to as Manila hemp even though it is not a true hemp (see Figure 5–6).

SISAL AND HENEQUEN

Sisal and *henequen* are closely related plants. They are grown in Africa, Central America, and the West Indies. Both fibers are smooth, straight, and yellow. They are used for better grades of rope, twine, and brush bristles. However, since both fibers are degraded by salt

Fig. 5–6 *Abaca place mat.*

water, they are not used in maritime ropes. In addition to these end uses, sisal may be substituted for horsehair in upholstery.

Wool and Other Animal-Hair Fibers

Natural protein fibers are of animal origin. Wool and specially wool ... the hair and fur of animals and silk ... the secretion of the silkworm ... natural protein fibers are prestige fibers to ... nay silk, ... cashmere and camel's hair have always been ... this category. Wool is still ... as it was through the 1960s ... Angora hair fibers will be discussed in this chapter. Silk will be discussed in Chapter 7.

Protein fibers are composed of various amino acids that have been formed in nature into polypeptide chains with high molecular weight. They contain the elements carbon, hydrogen, oxygen, and nitrogen. Wool, in addition, contains sulfur. Protein fibers are amphoteric, having both acidic and basic reactive groups. The protein of wool is keratin, whereas that of silk is fibroin.

The following is a simple formula for an amino acid:

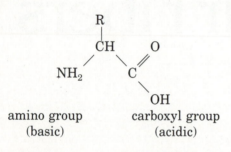

| amino group | carboxyl group |
| (basic) | (acidic) |

Protein fibers have some properties in common because of their chemical composition. These properties are important because they indicate the care required for the fabrics. Silk and wool have some different properties because their physical and molecular structures are different (see the following chart).

Properties	Importance to Consumer
Resiliency	Resist wrinkling. Wrinkles hang out between wearings. Fibers tend to return to original shape.
Hygroscopic	Comfortable in cool, damp climate. Moisture prevents buildup of ... in carpets.
Weaker when wet	Handle carefully during washing. Wool loses about 40 percent of its strength and silk loses about 15 percent.
Specific gravity	Fabrics feel lighter than cellulosics of the same thickness.
Harmed by alkali	Use neutral or slightly alkaline soap or detergent. Perspiration weakens the fiber.
Harmed by oxidizing agents	Chlorine bleaches damage fiber so should not be used. Sunlight causes white fabrics to turn yellowish.
Harmed by dry heat	Wool becomes harsh and brittle and scorches easily with dry heat. Use steam! White silk and wool turn yellow.
Flame resistance	Do not burn readily; are self-extinguishing; have odor of burning hair; and form a black, crushable ash.

Wool

Wool was one of the first fibers to be spun into yarns and woven into cloth. Wool and flax were the most widely used textile fibers when fibers were spun by hand before the Industrial Revolution.

Now, many people consider both wool and silk to be luxury fibers. Designers continue to use these fibers extensively in their collections. The consumer is most likely to have a wool sweater, suit, or coat. The high initial cost of wool products and the cost of their care have led many customers to classify wool garments as investment clothing. These factors have encouraged the substitution of acrylic, polyester, or blends of wool with these fibers in many end-use products.

In the 1960s, when man-made fibers were used in increasing amounts in sweaters, blankets, carpeting, and in many kinds of outerwear, wool was promoted as Nature's Wonder Fiber by the Wool Bureau. This is an apt description of wool. Wool has a combination of properties that are unequaled by any man-made fiber; namely, ability to be shaped by heat and moisture, ability to absorb moisture in vapor form without feeling wet, comfortable warmth in cold weather, initial water repellency, feltability, and flame retardance.

Sheep were probably the first animals domesticated by man. The covering of primitive sheep consisted of two parts: a long, hairy outercoat that was used primarily for rugs and felt, and a light, downy undercoat that was very desirable for clothing. The fleece of present-day domesticated sheep is primarily the soft undercoat. It is thought that cross breeding sheep to increase the amount of undercoat began about A.D. 100. By A.D. 1400, the Spanish had developed the Merino sheep, whose fleece contains no hair or kemp fiber. Kemp is a coarse, brittle, dead-white fiber found in the fleece of primitive sheep and still found in the wools of all breeds of sheep except the Merino.

Sheep were not known to the American Indian, before the Spanish brought sheep to the southwest in the 16th century. The sheep of the Navajo are descendants of an unimproved long-haired breed introduced during the 16th or 17th century.

Sheep raising on the Atlantic seaboard began in the Jamestown, Virginia, colony in 1609 and in the Massachusetts settlements in 1630. From these centers, the sheep-raising industry spread rapidly because it was vital to the welfare of the colonists. In 1643, twenty families of wool combers and carders emigrated from England, settled in the Massachusetts Bay colony, and produced and finished wool fabric.

Most textiles were imported until 1650, when the movement towards self-sufficiency in fabric production became strong. Following the Civil War, the opening of free grazing lands west of the Mississippi prepared the way for sheep raising on a larger scale than was possible on Eastern farms. There were 50 million range sheep by 1884; that year was the high point of sheep production in the United States. During the 1950s and 1960s, the sheep population was around 32 million. In the 1980s, it has further declined to 9 million.

PRODUCTION

In 1983–84, Australia produced 25 percent of the world's wool supply. It was followed by the Soviet Union (16 percent), New Zealand (12 per-

Fig. 6–1 *Merino sheep. (Courtesy of Australian Wool Corp.)*

cent), China (7 percent), and Argentina (6 percent). The United States ranked tenth, producing only 1.6 percent of the world supply.

Merino sheep produce the most valuable wool (Fig. 6–1). About 43 percent of merino wool comes from Australia. Good quality ewes produce 15 pounds of wool per fleece, while rams produce 20 pounds. Australian Merino wool is 3–5 inches long and very fine.

Fine wool is produced in the United States by four breeds of sheep: Delaine-Merino, Rambouillet, Debouillet, and Targhee (Fig. 6–2). More than half of this fine wool is produced in Texas and California. It is 2½–5 inches long.

Sheep are raised in every state of the United States, with the exception of Hawaii, but most

Fig. 6–2 *Rambouillet ewes. (Courtesy of the Texas Department of Agriculture. Photographer: Dan Morrison.)*

sheep are raised in Texas (18 percent) and California (11 percent). Wyoming, Colorado, South Dakota, and seven other western states are important producers (43 percent). The remaining 28 percent of sheep are raised in the East, South, and Midwest.

The greatest share of U.S. wool production is of medium-grade wools. These fibers have a larger diameter than the fine wools and a greater variation in length, from 1½–6 inches. There are 15 breeds of sheep commonly found in the United States. The breeds vary tremendously in appearance, type of wool produced, and other uses—such as meat, fat, and milk.

Sheep are generally sheared once a year in the spring. The fleece is removed with power shears that look like large barber's shears. A good shearer can handle 100–225 sheep per day. An expert can shear a sheep in less than 5 minutes. Shearers start in the Southern states in February and work northward, finishing in June.

The fleece is removed with long, smooth strokes, beginning at the legs and belly. A good shearer will leave the fleece in one piece. After shearing, the fleece is folded together and put in bags to be shipped to market.

At this point the wool is called *raw wool,* or *grease wool,* and it contains impurities such as sand and dirt, grease and dried sweat (called *suint*), which account for 30–70 percent of the weight of the fleece. Once these impurities are removed, the wool is called *clean,* or *scoured, wool.* The grease is a valuable byproduct; in its purified state, it is known as *lanolin* and is used in manufacturing face cream, cosmetics, soaps, and ointments.

Pulled wool is obtained from animals that are sold for meat. The pelts are washed and brushed, then treated chemically to loosen the fibers.

Grading and sorting are two marketing operations that put wools of like character together. In *grading,* the whole fleece is judged for fineness and length. Each fleece contains more than one quality of wool. In *sorting,* the individual fleece is pulled apart into sections of different-quality fibers. The best-quality wool comes from the sides, shoulders, and back, while the poorest wool comes from the lower legs.

Different qualities of wool are required for a particular product. For example, fine wool may be used in a lightweight worsted fabric while a coarse wool could be used in a bulky sweater.

The end use of the product determines the grade of wool required.

Quality of apparel wool is based on fineness and length and does *not* necessarily imply durability because fine fibers are not as durable as coarse fibers. Fineness, color, crimp, strength, length, and elasticity are wool-fiber characteristics that vary with the breed of the sheep.

TYPES AND KINDS

Many different qualities of wool are available for the production of yarns and fabrics. As mentioned before, wool from Merino sheep is a very high-quality wool. Breeds of sheep produce fibers with different characteristics. Labels on wool garments almost never give information about the breed of sheep; the fiber is simply identified as wool. Wool is the fleece of the sheep. The term *wool* legally includes fiber from the Angora goat, Cashmere goat, camel, alpaca, llama, and vicuña. Wool comes from several sources:

· Sheared wool—from live sheep
· Pulled wool—from the pelts of meat-type sheep
· Recycled wool—from worn clothing and cutters' scraps

Wool is often blended with less-expensive fibers to reduce the cost of the fabric or to extend its use. Congress passed the Wool Products Labeling Act in 1939 (amended in 1980) to protect consumers as well as producers, manufacturers, and distributors from the unrevealed presence of substitutes and mixtures and to inform the consumer of the source of the wool fiber. The law requires that the label must give the fiber content in terms of percent and also give the source. The act does *not* state anything about the quality. The consumer must rely on feel and texture to determine quality.

The terms that appear on the label of a garment made of wool fiber are defined by the Federal Trade Commission as follows:

1. Wool—new wool or wool fibers reclaimed from knit scraps, broken thread, and noils. (Noils are the short fibers that are combed out in the making of worsted yarns.)

2. Recycled wool—scraps of new woven or felted fabrics are *garnetted* (shredded) back to the fibrous state and used again in the manufacture of woolens. Wool (shoddy) from old clothing and rags are cleaned and sorted and shredded into fibers. Recycled wool is often blended with new wool before being respun. It is usually used in interlinings and mackinaw-type fabrics that are thick and boardy.

Recycled wool is important in the textile industry. However, these fibers lose some of the desirable properties of new wool during the wool-garnetting process. Some fibers are broken by the mechanical action and/or wear. The fibers are not as resilient, strong, or durable as new wool, yet the fabrics made from them perform very well.

The term *virgin wool* on a label does *not* necessarily mean good quality. The term is not defined by the law but has been defined by the Federal Trade Commission as wool that has never been processed in any way. This eliminates knit clips and broken threads from being labeled as virgin wool.

Lamb's wool comes from animals less than 7 months old and is finer and softer because it is the first shearing and the fiber has only one cut end; the other end is the natural tip (Figure 6–3). The term lamb's wool usually identifies it on a label.

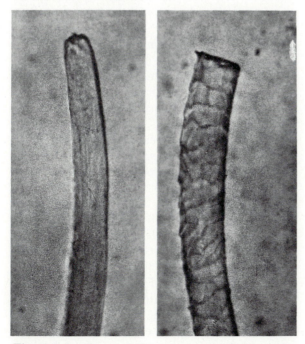

Fig. 6–3 *Lamb's wool fiber: natural tip* (left); *cut tip* (right).

PHYSICAL STRUCTURE

Length. The length of Merino wool fibers ranges from 1½ to 5 inches, depending on the kind of animal and the length of time between shearings. Long, fine wool fibers, used for worsted yarns and fabrics, have an average length of 2½ inches. The shorter fibers, which average 1½ inches in length, are used in woolen fabrics. Certain breeds of sheep produce coarse, long wools that measure from 5–15 inches in length. These long wools are used in specialty fabrics and hand weaving.

The diameter of wool fiber varies from 10–50 micrometers. Merino lamb's wool may average 15 micrometers in diameter. The wool fiber is made up of a cuticle, cortex, and medulla (Figure 6–4).

Medulla. When it is present, the *medulla* is a honeycomb-like core containing air spaces that increase the insulating power of the fiber. It appears as a dark area when seen through the microscope, but is usually absent in fine wools.

Cortex. The *cortex* is the main part of the fiber. It is made up of long, flattened, cigar-shaped cells with a nucleus near the center. In natural-colored wools, the cortical cells contain *melanin*, a colored pigment.

The cortical cells on the two sides of the wool fiber have somewhat different chemical and physical properties; they react differently to moisture and temperature. They are responsible for the three-dimensional crimp, which is

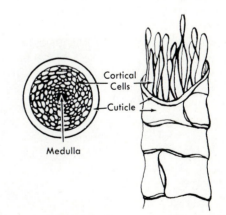

Fig. 6–4 *Physical structure of wool fibers. (Courtesy of Werner von Bergen from* Industrial and Engineering Chemistry, *September 1952; reprinted by permission.)*

unique to the wool fiber. Figure 6–5 shows the crimp in wool fiber. Fine Merino wool may have as many as 30 crimps per inch. Lower-quality wools may have as few crimps as 1–5 per inch. The irregular lengthwise waviness gives wool fabrics three very important properties: cohesiveness, elasticity, and loft. Crimp helps individual fibers cling together in a yarn; this cohesiveness increases the strength of the yarn over what one would expect from a low-strength fiber. Elasticity is increased—crimp makes the fiber act like a spring. As force is exerted on the fiber, the fiber first straightens out from its naturally wavy state to a flat state, without any damage to the fiber. Once the force is released, the wool fiber gradually will return to its crimped position. Crimp also is an important factor in the loft that wool fabrics exhibit. Because of the crimp of the fibers, yarns and fabrics made from wool are lofty or bulky and retain this loftiness throughout use. Two-dimensional crimp, or waviness, could be diagrammed like this: ◠◡◠◡. Figure 6–6, shows wool with crimp having this appearance.

Actually, the crimp in wool is three dimensional. The fiber itself turns even as it goes up and down in waves. Another way of saying this is that the fiber twists around its axis. This is drawn in Figure 6–6. Remember that the cortical cells on the two different sides of the fiber react differently to heat and moisture. Because wool has these two different parts, it is called a *natural bicomponent fiber*. To illustrate this bicomponent nature, think how a wool fiber will react to water. One side of the fiber will swell more than the other side; this will cause a de-

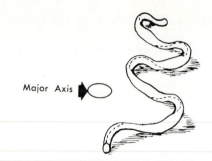

Fig. 6–6 *Three-dimensional crimp of wool fiber. (From G. E. Hopkins,* Wool As An Apparel Fiber. *Copyright 1953 by Holt, Rinehart and Winston, Inc.)*

crease in the natural crimp of the fiber. When the fiber dries, the crimp will return.

Wool has been described as a giant molecular coil spring with outstanding resiliency. This *resiliency* is excellent when the fiber is dry and poor when it is wet. If dry fabric is crushed in the hand, it tends to spring back to its original shape when the hand is opened. The wool fiber can be stretched to as much as 30 percent of its original length. When stress is applied, the waves and bends of the fiber straighten out, and when stress is removed, the fibers recover their original length. Recovery takes place more slowly when the fabric is dry. Steam, humidity, and water hasten recovery. This is why a wool garment will lose its wrinkles more rapidly when it is hung over a bathtub of steamy water.

Cuticle. The cuticle is made up of an epicuticle and a horny, nonfibrous layer of scales. The *epicuticle* is a thin, nonprotein membrane that covers the scales. This layer gives water repellency to the fiber, but is easily damaged by mechanical treatment. In fine wools, the *scales* completely encircle the shaft and each scale overlaps the bottom of the preceding scale like parts of a telescope. In medium and coarse wools, the scale arrangement resembles shingles on a roof or scales on a fish (Figure 6–7). The free edges of the scales project outward and point toward the tip of the fiber. They cause skin irritation for some people. The scale covering gives wool its abrasion resistance and felting property.

Felting, a unique and important property of wool, is based on the scale structure of the fiber. Under mechanical action, such as agitation, friction, and pressure in the presence of heat and moisture, the wool fiber tends to move rootward and the edges of the scales interlock, thus pre-

Fig. 6–5 *Natural crimp in wool fiber.*

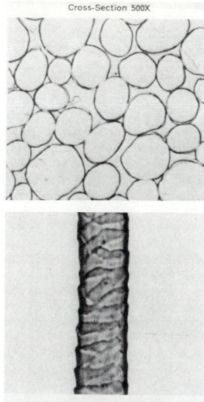

Cross-Section 500X

Longitudinal View 500X

Fig. 6–7 *Photomicrographs of wool. (Courtesy of American Association of Textile Chemists and Colorists.)*

venting the fiber from returning to its original position in the fabric. The result is the shrinkage, or felting, of the cloth.

Movement of the fibers is speeded up and felting occurs more rapidly under extreme or severe conditions. A wool garment can be shrunk down to half its original size. Lamb's wool will felt more readily than other wool. In soft, fluffy fabrics the fibers are not firmly held in position and are free to move, so these fabrics are more susceptible to felting than are the firmly woven worsteds. The felting property is an advantage in making felt fabric directly from fibers without spinning or weaving. The felting property is a disadvantage because it makes the laundering of wool more difficult. Treatments to prevent felting shrinkage (see Chapter 34) are based on the principle of smoothing off the rough edges of the scales.

Fulling, or *milling,* is a cloth-finishing process in which the cloth is washed in a thick soap solution and squeezed by wooden rollers to shrink the cloth and close up the weave by bringing the yarns closer together. After fulling, the cloth has more body and cover, as shown in Figure 6–8. The shrinking is dependent on the action of heat and moisture on the molecule structure and also on the scale structure. *Fulling, the process, should not be confused with felting, the property.*

Fig. 6–8 *Wool cloth before* (left) *and after* (right) *fulling.*

CHEMICAL COMPOSITION AND MOLECULAR ARRANGEMENT

Wool fiber is a protein called *keratin*. It is the same protein that is found in human hair, fingernails, horns, and hooves. Keratin is made up of carbon, hydrogen, oxygen, nitrogen, and sulfur. These combine to form over 17 different amino acids. Five amino acids are shown in Figure 6–9. The individual wool molecule consists of flexible molecular chains held together by natural crosslinks—cystine (or sulfur) linkages and salt bridges.

Figure 6–9 somewhat resembles a ladder, with the crosslinks analogous to the cross bars of the ladder. This simple structure can be useful in understanding some of the properties of wool. Imagine a ladder made of plastic that is pulled askew. When wool is pulled, its inherent tendency is to recover is original shape; the crosslinks are very important in this recovery. However, if the crosslinks are damaged, the structure is destroyed and recovery cannot occur.

A more-realistic model of the structure of wool molecules would have this ladder-like structure alternating with a helical structure. About 40 percent of the chains are in a spiral formation, with hydrogen bonding occurring between the closer parts. The ladder-like formation occurs where cystine crosslinks are or where other bulky amino acids mean the chains cannot pack closely together. The spiral formation works like a spring and is also important in the resilience, elongation, and elastic recovery of wool fibers. Figure 6–10 shows the helical structure of wool.

The cystine linkage is the most important part of the molecule. Any chemical, such as alkali, that damages this linkage can destroy the entire structure. In controlled reactions, the linkage can be broken and then reformed. Minor modifications of the cystine linkage that result from ironing and steaming have a beneficial effect; those from careless washing and exposure to light have a detrimental effect.

Shaping of Wool Fabrics. Wool fabrics can be shaped by heat and moisture—a definite aid in tailoring. Puckers can be pressed out; excess fabric can be eased and then pressed flat or rounded as desired. Pleats can be pressed into wool cloth with heat, steam, and pressure, but they will not last through washing.

Hydrogen bonds are broken by moisture and heat so the wool structure can be re-shaped by the mechanical action of the iron or press. Simultaneously, the heat dries the wool and new hydrogen bonds are formed in the wool structure as the water escapes as steam. The new hydrogen bonds maintain the wool in the new shape so long as the humidity is low. In high humidity or if the wool is dampened with water, the new hydrogen bonds are broken and the molecular structure reverts to its former shape. This is why garments shaped by ironing lose their creases or flatness and show relaxation shrinkage on wetting.—"What Happens When Setting Wool," Textile Industries, *130 (October 1966): 344.*

Permanent "set" can be achieved in much the same way and by chemicals similar to those used in the permanent waving of hair. The Si-Ro-Set finish, developed in Australia, uses the chemical ammonium thyglycollate. The fabric is sprayed or soaked with the chemical and then set as pleats or the like by steaming or steam pressing for a required period of time. During setting, the cystine linkage splits between the two sulfur atoms and new linkages are formed.

Wool fabrics are *subject to shrinkage*. The somewhat amorphous molecular structure of wool permits water molecules to penetrate, and,

Summary of the Performance of Wool in Apparel Fabrics

AESTHETIC	*VARIABLE*
Luster	Matte
DURABILITY	*HIGH*
Abrasion resistance	Moderate
Tenacity	Low
Elongation	High
COMFORT	*HIGH*
Absorbency	High
Thermal retention	High
APPEARANCE RETENTION	*HIGH*
Resiliency	High
Dimensional stability	Low
Elastic recovery	Excellent
RECOMMENDED CARE	*DRY CLEAN*

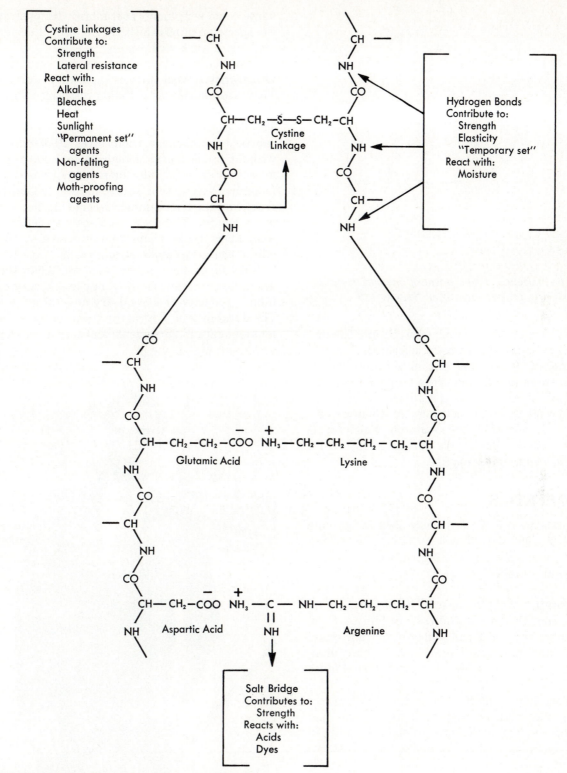

Fig. 6–9 Structural formula of the wool molecule.

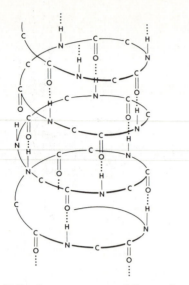

Fig. 6–10 *Helical arrangement of the wool molecule. (Courtesy of International Wool Secretariat.)*

when they do, the wool fiber swells and the molecular chains can be easily deformed.

Another finish that minimizes the effect of moisture in laundering is the Wurlan finish, developed by the Western Utilization Research and Development Laboratory at Albany, California. A polyamide-type solution, which forms a microscopic film on the surface of the scales and masks them, is applied.

PROPERTIES

One slogan the Wool Bureau used to promote wool in 1985 was "Wool . . . Good Looks That Last." Wool garments look good, wear well, and are comfortable.

Aesthetic. Wool, because of its physical structure, contributes loft and body to fabrics. Wool sweaters and men's and women's suit fabrics are the standard "looks" by which similar man-made fiber fabrics are measured. (See Figure 6–11.)

Wool has a matte appearance. Fibers are sometimes blended with wool from sheep that produce longer fibers or with specialty hair fibers such as mohair to make more-lustrous fabrics.

Drape, texture, and hand can be varied by choice of yarn structure, fabric structure, and finish. Sheer-wool scarves, medium-weight drapey printed-wool challis, medium-weight suit fabrics for summer, heavyweight suit fabrics for winter, and very heavy coat fabrics demonstrate the spectrum of possibilities. No wonder designers love to work with wool!

Durability. Wool fabrics are very durable. They have moderate abrasion resistance due to the scale structure of the fiber and its flexibility. The flexibility of wool is excellent. Wool fibers can be bent back on themselves 20,000 times without breaking, as compared to 3,000 times for cotton and 75 times for rayon. Atmospheric moisture helps wool to retain its flexibility. Wool carpets, for example, become brittle if the air is too dry. The crimp and scale structure of wool fibers make them very cohesive so they cling together to make strong yarns.

Wool fibers have a low tenacity. When they are pulled lengthwise until they break, they exhibit a tenacity of 1.5 g/d dry and 1.0 g/d wet. The durability of wool is the result of the excellent elongation (25 percent) and elastic recovery

Fig. 6–11 *Man's business suit made from wool. (Courtesy of Gant Clothing.)*

(99 percent) of the fibers. When stress is put on the fabric, the crimped fibers elongate, then the molecular chains unfold. When stress is removed, the crosslinks pull the fibers back almost to their original positions. The combination of these properties, excellent flexibility, elongation, and elastic recovery, results in wool fabrics that can be used and enjoyed for many years.

Comfort. Wool is more hygroscopic than any other fiber. It has a moisture regain of from 13–18 percent under standard conditions. All animal fibers are superior to other fibers in that they absorb moisture without surface wetting; they are *hygroscopic*. This phenomenon has long been recognized as a major factor in understanding why garments made from protein fibers are so comfortable to wear. Hygroscopic fibers minimize sudden temperature changes at the skin. This is illustrated by the difference in warmth between an all-polyester suit and an all-wool suit. In the winter, when people go from a dry indoor atmosphere into the damp outdoor air, the wool fibers absorb moisture and generate heat, protecting the wearers from the cold.

Outdoor-sports enthusiasts have long recognized the superior comfort provided by wool. After a period of activity, no sudden chilling occurs when exercise stops because the wool fiber absorbs moisture and releases heat. The process of the wool slowly drying and the moisture evaporating into the air occurs slowly enough that the wearer is more comfortable than in any other fiber.

Wool fibers are initially water repellent. In a light rain or snow, the water will run off or remain on the fabric surface. In a heavier rain, wool will absorb a lot of moisture without feeling wet. Eventually wool will absorb enough moisture so that it will feel wet and heavy.

Wool is a poor conductor of heat so that warmth from the body is not dissipated readily. Wool's excellent resiliency is important in providing warmth. The wool fibers can recover from crushing and the fabrics will remain porous and capable of incorporating much air. "Still" air is one of the best insulators because it keeps body heat close to the body.

Coarse-wool fabrics are often irritating to the skin. Some people are allergic to the chemical components of wool and itch or break out in a rash or sneeze when they wear or handle wool. Fabrics that seem scratchy may be a low-quality

wool. Feel them and try them on before purchasing. Wear them layered with a smooth fabric underneath them or try some better-quality fabrics.

Wool has a medium density (1.32 g/cc). People often associate heavy fabrics with wool since it is used in fall and winter wear when the additional warmth given by heavy fabrics is desirable. Lightweight wools are very comfortable in the changeable temperatures of spring and early fall.

One way to compare fiber densities is to think of blankets. A winter blanket of wool is heavy and warm. An equally thick blanket of cotton would be even heavier (cotton has a higher density), but not as warm. A winter blanket of acrylic would be lighter in weight (acrylic has a lower density than either). Personal preferences, room temperature, and humidity need to be considered before deciding which fiber content would be more comfortable.

Appearance Retention. Wool is a very resilient fiber. It resists wrinkling and recovers well from wrinkles. It wrinkles more readily when wet. Wool maintains its shape fairly well during normal use. Women's slacks and straight skirts should be lined to prevent baggy knees or saggy seats. Men's worsted suiting fabrics are designed to retain their shape well.

When wool fabrics are dry cleaned, they retain their size and shape well. When wool sweaters are hand washed, they need to be cared for properly to avoid shrinking. Follow care instructions for washable woolens.

Wool has an excellent elastic recovery—99 percent at 2 percent elongation. Even at 20 percent elongation, recovery is 63 percent. Recovery is excellent from the stresses of normal usage. The fabric regains its shape best when allowed to rest at least 24 hours between wearings.

Care. Wool does not soil readily, and the removal of soil from wool is relatively simple. Grease and oils do not spot wool fabrics as readily as they do fabrics made of other fibers. (Wool in its natural state is about 25 percent grease). Wool garments do not need to be washed or dry cleaned after every wearing. They do not wrinkle very much. They can be spot treated. Layer them with a washable shirt to decrease odor pickup.

Use a good brush on collars and the inside of cuffs after each wearing. A firm, soft brush not only removes dust but also gently lifts the fibers back to their natural springiness. Damp fabrics should be allowed to dry before brushing. Garments should have a period of rest between wearings to recover from deformations. Baggy elbows and skirt seats will become less baggy as the garment rests. Hanging the garment over a tub of hot, steamy water or spraying a fine mist of water on the cloth will speed up recovery.

Wool is very weak when it is wet. Its wet tenacity is 1.0 g/d, a third lower than its relatively low dry strength. Wet elongation increases to 35 percent before breaking. Resiliency and elastic recovery decrease when wool is wet. The redeeming properties of dry wool that make it durable in spite of its low tenacity do not operate when it is wet. Wet wool is weak; handle it very gently.

Dry cleaning is the recommended method of caring for wool garments. Dry cleaning minimizes the potential problems that may occur during hand or machine washing. The cost of dry cleaning may be viewed as a disadvantage and needs to be evaluated on an individual basis. The dry cleaner removes spots and stains, does minor repairs, cleans the garment, steam presses it, and can also store it. For many people, the convenience of these services is worth the cost. Incorrect care procedures can be disastrous and costly; the garment can be ruined so it can no longer be worn.

Follow care instructions. Dry cleaning is always appropriate for wool garments. Knit sweaters can be dry cleaned or they can be hand washed if correct procedures are followed. When hand washing, warm water that is comfortable to the hand is recommended. Avoid agitation; squeeze gently. Support the garment, especially if it is knit, so it does not stretch unnecessarily. Fabrics and garments, woven or knit, that are labeled machine washable are usually fiber blends or have been given a special finish so they can be laundered safely. Follow any special instructions given. These special instructions usually include warm or lukewarm water and a gentle cycle for a short period of time, with line drying or flat drying.

Chlorine bleach will damage wool. Verify this by putting a small piece of wool in fresh chlorine bleach (bleach gets weaker with age). What happens? The wool dissolves! This can be used as a simple test to identify protein fibers. Chlorine bleach is an oxidizing agent. Wool is also very sensitive to the action of alkali. The wool reacts to the alkali by turning yellow, then becoming slick and jelly-like, and finally going into solution. If the fabric is a blend, the wool in the blend will disintegrate, leaving only the other fibers.

Avoid using the dryer for wool clothing or blankets. If care instructions state to machine dry, use a low-temperature setting and remove the garment while it is still slightly damp to the touch, letting it finish drying flat.

Following these care procedures will prevent extreme shrinkage. Under conditions of heat, moisture, agitation, and pressure, wool will felt—the fibers will shorten and their scales will lock together in an irreversible process. If an adult-sized sweater is carelessly machine washed for an average length of time with regular agitation and then dried in a hot dryer, it will be child-sized and very stiff when it is removed.

Use care in ironing wool apparel. Wool becomes weak and harsh at elevated temperatures, and it scorches readily. Wool fabrics should always be pressed with moist heat.

If wool fabrics become shiny from pressure, sponge with a 5 percent solution of white vinegar. Then steam, and the fibers will swell and become fluffier. If surface fibers wear off, use fine sandpaper to restore the nap. Fine sandpaper will also remove *light* scorch.

Wool is attacked by moth larvae and other insects. The most effective way to prevent moth damage to wool is to alter the molecular structure of the fiber. The mothproofing process consists of chemically breaking the cystine linkage ($-S-S-$) and reforming it as $-S-CH_2-S-$ (see Chapter 34).

Unless mothproofed, wool fabrics should be stored so that they will not be accessible to moths. Moth larvae will also eat, but not digest, any fiber that is blended with wool. Wool fabrics should be cleaned before storage and should be stored with moth crystals in a closed container.

Wool burns very slowly and is self-extinguishing. It is normally regarded as flame-resistant. When used for curtains, carpets, and upholstery in trains, planes, ships, hotels, and other public buildings, wool is often given a flame-retardant finish.

When wool burns, it gives off only moderate

amounts of smoke and carbon monoxide and is a minor impediment to evacuation from the site of a fire as compared to other materials that are likely to be present. The temporary resistance to burning of wool may be increased by the use of phosphates or borates. Durable fire-retardant effects can be obtained by the use of small amounts of a variety of protective compounds with little detectable change in the physical or chemical behavior of the wool fiber.

USES

Only a small amount of wool is used in the United States. Domestic consumption of wool was 195 million pounds, or 1.7 percent of all fiber used in the United States in 1985. A greater amount of wool is imported than is produced domestically.

The majority of wool (72.8 percent) is used in apparel. Home furnishings account for 15.4 percent, industrial uses 6.7 percent, and exports 5 percent. Wool accounts for 3.3 percent of all fibers used for apparel.

The most important use of wool is for adult apparel: coats, jackets, suits, dresses, skirts, and slacks made from woven fabrics of varying weights; and suits, dresses, skirts, and sweaters made from knitted fabrics. In the early 1980s, there was a trend towards greater consumption of women's suits containing wool. Manufacturers tried to develop a greater variety of women's suiting fabrics to meet this demand.

Uses of Wool in 1985

Percent	End Use	Million Pounds
72.8	Apparel	
	Top weight	2.7
	Bottom weight	105.7
	Underwear and nightwear	3.9
	Sweaters	16.8
	Retail piece goods	2.9
	Socks	2.7
	Hand-knitting yarns	4.3
15.4	Home Furnishing	
	Carpets	11.9
	Upholstery	13.6
	Blankets	4.1
6.7	Industrial	
	Felts	12.1

Source: Textile Organon, 57 (9), Sept. 1986.

Performance standards are stricter for menswear than for womenswear. Wool suits perform very well and look great. They fit well because they can be shaped through tailoring. The fabrics hang well. The suits last a long time. They are very comfortable under a variety of conditions and retain their good looks during wear and care. Suits are typically dry cleaned to retain their best looks and because of the shaping components.

Blends of different synthetic fibers with wool for suiting materials are increasingly important. They result in fabrics that are more appropriate in warmer conditions. Polyester is the most important fiber used. Varying percentages of wool and polyester are used. Other fibers may also be used; sometimes two or three synthetics are blended with wool.

Wool is important in knitwear—especially sweaters. Wool is also used in retail piece goods, socks, and hand-knitting yarns.

In 1964, the Wool Bureau adopted the Woolmark as a symbol of quality to be used on all merchandise that meets the Wool Bureau's specifications for quality. In 1970—recognizing the increasing use of blends—the Wool Bureau adopted a Woolblend mark for blends with at least 60 percent wool. The Woolmark and Woolblend symbols are shown in Figure 6–12.

In the home-furnishing area, the major use of wool is in carpets and rugs. Many woven Axminster and Wilton rugs with Persian-type designs are made from wool. More contemporary looks are also available. Most are imported, although some are made in the United States. Wool rugs are more expensive than nylon carpets, but people who prefer them like the pat-

PURE WOOL   WOOLBLEND
                   MARK

Fig. 6–12 *Woolmark® and Woolblend® symbols of quality. (Courtesy of the Wool Bureau, Inc.)*

terns and appreciate the color, texture, and appearance of wool. Wool rugs account for a very small share of the rug market. Wool is also found in upholstery fabrics and blankets.

In industrial uses, wool is important in felts. These are used under heavy machinery to help decrease noise or for a variety of other uses.

Specialty Hair Fibers

Most specialty wools are obtained from the goat, rabbit, and camel families.

Specialty wools are available in smaller quantities than sheep's wool so they are usually more expensive. Like all natural fibers, wools vary in quality.

Specialty wool fibers are of two kinds: the coarse long outerhair and the soft, fine undercoat. Coarse fibers are used for interlinings, upholstery, and some coatings; the very fine fibers are used in luxury coatings, sweaters, shawls, suits, and dress fabrics.

MOHAIR

Mohair is the hair fiber of the Angora goat. In 1985, 41.4 million pounds of mohair were produced worldwide. South Africa produced the most (38 percent), followed by Turkey (29 percent) and the United States (24 percent). Texas is the major producer in the United States. Most U.S. mohair (80 percent of it) is exported to the United Kingdom, with smaller amounts going to South Africa and Italy. The goats (Figure 6–13) are sheared twice a year, in the early fall and early spring. The fiber length is

· 4–6 inches for half a year
· 8–12 inches for a full year

Mohair fibers have a circular cross-section. Scales on the surface are scarcely visible and the cortical cells show through as lengthwise striations. There are some air ducts between the cells that give mohair its lightness and fluffiness. Few of the fibers have a medulla.

Mohair is one of the most resilient fibers and has none of the crimp found in sheep's wool, giving it a silk-like luster and a smoother surface that is more resistant to dust than wool. Mohair has fewer scales than wool, so mohair fibers are smoother than wool fibers. (Figure 6–14). Mohair is very strong and has good affinity for dye. The washed fleece is a lustrous white.

Chemical properties are the same as those of wool. Mohair makes a better novelty *loop* yarn than wool or the other specialty hair fibers.

Uses of Mohair

· Upholstery and draperies
· Men's suitings
· Bouclé coatings for women
· Pile fabrics; embossed and curled like fur
· Laces
· Wigs and hairpieces
· Oriental-type rugs

Figure 6–15 is the quality symbol used on all mohair products that meet performance standards established by the Mohair Council.

QIVIUT

Qiviut, a rare and luxurious fiber, is the underwool of the domesticated musk ox. See Fig. 6–16. Successful domestication projects have been conducted in Alaska. A large musk ox will provide 6 pounds of wool each year. The fiber can be used just as it comes from the animal, for it is protected from debris by the long guard hairs and has a low lanolin content. The fleece is not shorn but is shed naturally and is removed from the

Goat Family	Camel Family	Others
Angora goat—mohair	Camel's hair	Angora rabbit—angora
Cashmere goat—cashmere	Llama	Fur fibers
	Alpaca	Musk ox—qiviut
	Vicuña	
	Guanaco	

Fig. 6-13 *Angora goats produce mohair fibers. (Courtesy of the Mohair Council of America.)*

guard hairs as soon as it becomes visible. In 1984, qiviut was $125 an ounce.

Eskimo women hand knit with qiviut. Their first products were lacy scarves with designs taken from the Eskimo artifacts, and each pattern is identified with a particular village.

ANGORA

Angora is the hair on the angora rabbit, which is raised in France and in small amounts in the United States. See Figure 6-17. Each rabbit produces only a few ounces of fiber, which is very fine, fluffy, soft, slippery, and fairly long. It is pure white in color.

CAMEL'S HAIR

Camel's hair is obtained from the two-hump Bactrian camel. These camels are found in the area of Asia from Turkey east to China and north to Siberia. Camel's hair is said to have the

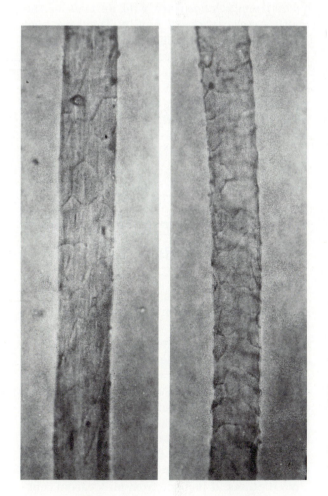

Mohair   Wool

Fig. 6-14 *Microscopic view of mohair and wool. (Courtesy of U.S.D.A., Livestock Division, Wool and Mohair Lab.)*

Fig. 6-16 *The musk ox of Alaska produces qiviut fiber. (Courtesy of Fairbanks Convention and Visitor Bureau.)*

Fig. 6–17 *The Angora rabbit produces a soft, white fiber. (Courtesy of Mary Goodwin.)*

best insulation of any of the wool fibers, since it keeps the camel comfortable under extreme conditions of temperature during a day's journey through the cold mountain passes and the hot valleys. The hair is collected by a "trailer" who follows the camel caravan and picks up the hair as it is shed and places it in a basket carried by the last camel. The trailer also gathers the hair in the morning, at the spot where the camels lay down for the night. A camel produces about 5 pounds of hair a year.

Because the camel's hair gives warmth without weight, the finer fibers are much prized for clothing fabrics. They are often used in blends with sheep's wool, which is dyed the tan color of camel's hair.

There are so many qualities of cashmere and camel's hair that care should be taken by consumers to determine the quality of fiber they are buying. The best way to judge the quality is by the feel. Consumers should be guided by the reputation of the manufacturer or retailer.

CASHMERE

Cashmere comes from a small goat raised in Kashmir, China, Tibet, and Mongolia. The fibers vary in color from white to gray to brownish gray. The goat has an outercoat of long, coarse hair and an innercoat of down. The hair is combed by hand from the animal during the molting season, and care is taken to separate the coarse hair from the fine fibers. Only a small part of the fleece is the very fine fiber, probably

not more than one-quarter pound per goat. Cashmere is used in high-quality apparel, especially women's sweaters and coatings. Fabrics are warm, buttery in hand, and have beautiful draping characteristics. Cashmere is more sensitive to chemicals than wool.

LLAMA AND ALPACA

Llama and *alpaca* are domesticated animals of the South American branch of the camel family. The fiber is 8–12 inches in length and is noted for its softness, fineness, and luster. The natural colors are white, light fawn, light brown, dark brown, gray, black, and piebald.

VICUÑA AND GUANACO

Vicuña and *guanaco* are wild animals of the South American camel family. They are very rare, and the animals must be killed to obtain the fiber. The governments of countries where vicuña and guanaco are found have limited the number of animals that can be harvested each year in order to protect the herds from extinction. Vicuña is the softest, finest, rarest, and most expensive of all textile fibers. The fiber is short, very lustrous, and a light-cinnamon color.

Azlon

Man-made protein fibers, *azlon*, are made by dissolving and resolidifying protein substances from animal or grain sources. They are no longer made in the United States. In the 1940s and 1950s, Aralac, made from milk casein, and Vicara, made from the zein of corn, were produced, but these fibers were not successful because they were too weak to be used alone and too expensive to compete with other blending fibers, particularly rayon and acetate.

Chinon is an azlon fiber that is presently manufactured in Japan and imported to the United States. It is made from milk casein combined with acrylic resins. Its characteristics are silk-like; it is used in scarves, ties, blouses, and sweaters. It is also used in the pharmaceutical industry.

7

Silk

Silk is a natural protein fiber. It is similar to wool in that it is composed of amino acids arranged in a polypeptide chain. Silk is produced by the larvae of a moth, while wool is produced by animals. All protein fibers have some general characteristics in common, such as their sensitivity to oxidizing agents and alkalis and their weaker strength when wet. Some characteristics differ significantly between the two fibers, such as the natural luster and uncrimped nature of silk.

Silk culture, according to Chinese legend, began in 2640 B.C. when a Chinese Empress Hsi Ling Shi became interested in silkworms and learned how to reel the silk and make it into fabric. It was through her efforts that China developed a silk industry that was monopolized for 3,000 years. Silk culture spread to Korea and Japan, westward to India and Persia, and then finally to Spain, France, and Italy. Silk fabrics, imported from China, were coveted by other countries; in India, the fabrics were often picked out and rewoven into looser fabrics or combined with linen to provide more yardage from the same amount of silk filament. Major producers of silk are Japan, Thailand, and the People's Republic of China.

Silk is universally accepted as a luxury fiber. The International Silk Association of the United States emphasizes the uniqueness of silk by its slogan "Only silk is silk." Silk has a unique combination of properties not possessed by any other fiber:

· "Dry" tactile hand
· Natural luster
· Good moisture absorption
· Lively suppleness and draping qualities
· High strength

The beauty and hand of silk and its high cost are probably responsible for the man-made fiber industry. In the early days, there was no scarcity of other natural fibers and thus no need to try to duplicate them. Silk is a solid fiber with a simple physical structure. It is this physical nature of silk that some modifications of man-made fibers (rayon and acetate) and synthetic fibers (nylon and polyester) attempt to duplicate. Man-made fibers with a triangular cross-section are the most successful.

PRODUCTION

Sericulture is the name given to the production of cultivated silk, which begins with the silk moth laying eggs on specially prepared paper. The cultivated silkworm is *Bombyx mori*. When the eggs hatch, the caterpillars, or larvae, are fed fresh, young mulberry leaves. After about 35 days and 4 moltings, the silkworms are approximately 10,000 times heavier than when born and ready to begin spinning a cocoon, or chrysalis case. A straw frame is placed on the tray and the silkworm starts to spin the cocoon by moving its head in a figure-eight (see Figure 7–1). The silkworm produces silk in two glands and forces the liquid silk through openings, called *spinnerets,* in its head. The two strands of silk are coated with a water soluble, protective gum called *sericin.* When the silk comes in contact with the air, it solidifies. In 2 or 3 days, the silkworm has spun approximately 1 mile of filament and has completely surrounded itself in a cocoon. The silkworm then begins to change into a chrysalis and then into a moth. Usually the silkworm is killed (stifled) with heat before it reaches the moth stage. If the silkworm is allowed to reach the moth stage, it will be used for breeding additional silkworms. The moth secretes a fluid that dissolves the silk at one end of the cocoon, permitting the moth to crawl out. Cocoons from which the moth has emerged cannot be used for filament silk yarns and the silk from these cocoons is not as valuable.

To obtain filament silk from the cocoon after the silkworm has been stifled, the cocoons are brushed to find the outside ends of the filaments.

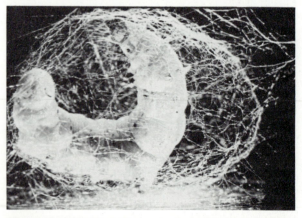

Fig. 7–1 *Silk caterpillar spinning silk fibers to form cocoon. (Courtesy of Stock, Boston. © Cary Wolinsky, 1984.)*

Several filaments are gathered together and wound onto a reel. This process is referred to as *reeling,* and it is performed in a manufacturing plant called a *filature.* Each cocoon yields approximately 1,000 yards of silk filament. This is *raw silk,* or *silk-in-the-gum.* Several filaments are combined to form a yarn. The operators in the filature must be careful to join the fibers so that the diameter of the reeled silk remains uniform in size. Uniformly reeled filament silk is the most valuable (see Figure 7–2).

As the fibers are combined and wrapped onto the reel, twist can be added to hold the filaments together. Adding twist is referred to as *throwing,* and the resulting yarn is called a *thrown yarn.* There are several types of thrown yarns. The type of yarn and amount of twist relate to the type of fabric desired. The simplest type of thrown yarn is a singles. In a *singles,* three to eight filaments are twisted together to form a yarn. Commonly used for filling yarns in many silk fabrics, singles may have two to three twists per inch.

Much usable silk is not reeled because long filaments cannot be taken from a damaged cocoon. Cocoons where the filament broke or where the moth was allowed to mature, and silk from the inner portions of the cocoon yield *silk noils,* or *silk waste.* This silk is degummed and spun as any other staple fiber or blended with another staple fiber and spun into a yarn. Spun silk is less expensive than filament silk.

Wild silk production is not controlled as it is for cultivated silk. Although many species of wild silkworms produce wild silk, the two most common species are *Antheraea mylitta* and *Antheraea pernyi.* The silkworms feed on oak and cherry leaves and produce fibers that are much less uniform in texture and color. The fiber may be brown, yellow, orange, or green, with brown the most common color for wild silk. Since the cocoons are harvested after the moth has matured, the silk cannot be reeled and must be used as spun silk. Wild silk is also referred to as *tussah silk.* It is coarser, darker, and cannot be bleached. Hence, white and light colors are not available in tussah silk.

Duppioni silk results when two silkworms spin their cocoons together. The yarn is irregular in diameter, with a thick-thin appearance, and used in linen-like silk fabrics for apparel.

FIBER PROPERTIES

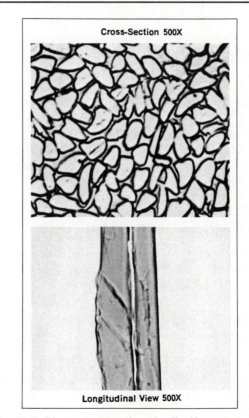

Cross-Section 500X

Longitudinal View 500X

Fig. 7–3 *Photomicrographs of silk fiber: cross-sectional view* (top); *longitudinal view* (bottom). *(Courtesy of American Association of Textile Chemists and Colorists.)*

Fig. 7–2 *Reeling of silk. (Courtesy of Stock, Boston. Photographer: Ira Kirschenbaum.)*

Summary of the Performance of Silk in Apparel Fabrics

AESTHETIC	VARIABLE
Luster	Beautiful and soft
DURABILITY	HIGH
Abrasion resistance	Moderate
Tenacity	High for natural fibers
Elongation	Moderate
COMFORT	HIGH
Absorbency	High
Thermal retention	Good
APPEARANCE RETENTION	MODERATE
Resiliency	Moderate
Dimensional stability	High
Elastic recovery	Moderate
RECOMMENDED CARE	DRY CLEAN

PHYSICAL STRUCTURE

Silk is a natural continuous-filament fiber. It is a solid fiber, smooth but irregular in diameter along its shaft. The filaments are triangular in cross-section with rounded corners (Figure 7–3). Silk fibers are very fine—1.25 denier/filament. Tussah silk may have slight striations along the longitudinal length of the fiber.

CHEMICAL COMPOSITION AND MOLECULAR STRUCTURE

The protein in silk is *fibroin,* which contains 15 amino acids in polypeptide chains. Silk has reactive amino (NH_2) and carboxyl (COOH) groups. Silk has no crosslinkages and no bulky side chains. The molecular chains are not folded as in wool, but are almost fully extended and packed closely together. Thus silk is highly oriented, which gives the fiber its strength. As with all fibers, there are some amorphous areas between the crystalline areas, giving silk its elasticity.

PROPERTIES

Aesthetic. Silk can be dyed and printed in brilliant colors. It is adaptable to a variety of fabrication methods. Thus it is available in a wide variety of fabric types. Because of cultivated silk's smooth but slightly irregular surface and triangular cross-section, the luster of this fiber is soft with an occasional sparkle. It is this luster that has been the model for many man-made fibers. Fabrics made of cultivated silk usually have a smooth appearance and a luxurious hand.

Tussah silk has a duller luster because of its coarser size, less-regular surface, and presence of sericin. Fabrics made of tussah silk have a more-pronounced texture.

In filament form, silk does not have good covering power. Before the development of strong synthetic fibers, silk was the only strong filament, and silk fabrics were often treated with metallic salts such as tin, a process called *weighting,* to give the fabric better drape, covering power, and dye absorption. Silk has *scroop,* a natural rustle, which can be increased by treating with an organic acid such as acetic or tartaric acid.

Durability. Silk has moderate abrasion resistance. Because of its end uses and cost, silk seldom receives harsh abrasion.

Silk is one of the strongest natural fibers, with a tenacity ranging from 3.5–5.0 g/d dry. It may lose up to 20 percent of its strength when wet. Its strength is excellent in relationship to its fineness.

Silk has a breaking elongation of 20 percent. It is not as elastic as wool because there are no crosslinkages to pull back the molecular chains. When silk is elongated by 2 percent, its elasticity is only 90 percent. Thus, when silk is stretched a small amount, it does not return to its original length, but remains slightly stretched. When silk is used in apparel, this poor elasticity may be seen in baggy elbows in blouses.

Comfort. Silk has good absorbency with a moisture regain of 11 percent. Silk is a poor conductor of electricity; thus problems may develop with static cling. Silk fabrics are comfortable in summer in skin-contact apparel. Silk, like wool, is a poor conductor of heat so that silk scarves and raw-silk suitings are comfortably warm in the winter. The weight of a fabric is important in heat conductivity—sheer fabrics, possible with filament silk, will be cool whereas heavy-suiting fabrics will be warm.

Silk is smooth and soft and thus not irritating to the skin.

The density of silk is 1.25 g/cc, which gives strength and light weight to silk products. Weighted silk is not as durable as regular silk, and it wrinkles more readily. In 1932, the Federal Trade Commission ruled that anything labeled pure silk or pure dye silk could contain no more than 15 percent weighting for black and 10 percent weighting for all other colors. Anything exceeding these levels is weighted silk. At present, very little silk is weighted.

Appearance Retention. Silk has moderate resistance to wrinkling. This is related to silk's elastic recovery. Because the fiber does not recover well from elongation, it does not resist wrinkling as well as some other fibers.

Silk fibers do not shrink. Because the molecular chains are not easily distorted, silk swells a small amount when wet. Fabrics made from true crepe yarns will shrink if laundered, but this is caused by the yarn structure, not the fiber content.

Care. Dry-cleaning solvents do not damage silk. In fact, dry cleaning often is recommended for silk items because of yarn structures, dyes that have poor fastness to water or laundering, or garment- or fabric-construction methods. Some silk items can be laundered in a mild detergent solution with gentle agitation. Since silk may lose up to 20 percent of it strength when wet, care should be taken with wet silks to avoid adding any unnecessary stress. Silk items should be pressed after laundering. Pure dye silks should be ironed damp with a press cloth. Wild silks should be dry cleaned and ironed dry to avoid losing sericin, which gives the fabric its body.

Silks may water-spot easily so care should be taken to avoid this problem. Before hand or machine washing, test in an obscure place of the item to make sure the dye does not water-spot.

Silk can be damaged and yellowed by strong soaps or detergents and high temperatures. Chlorine bleaches should be avoided. However, bleaches of hydrogen-peroxide and sodium-perborate are safe to use if the directions are followed carefully.

Silk is resistant to dilute mineral acids and organic acids, but it is damaged by strong alkaline solutions. A crepe-like surface effect may be created by the shrinking action of some acids.

Silk is weakened by exposure to sunlight and perspiration. Many dyes used to color silk are damaged by sunlight and perspiration. Silks tend to yellow with age and exposure to sunlight and chlorine bleach. Furnishing fabrics of silk should be protected from direct exposure to sunlight.

Silks may be attacked by insects, especially carpet beetles. Care should be taken when storing silks to be sure they are clean because soil may attract insects that do not normally attack silk.

Weighted silks deteriorate even under good storage conditions and are especially likely to break at folds. Historic items often exhibit a condition known as *shattered silk,* where the weighted silk is disintegrating. The process cannot be reversed.

Identification Tests. Silk burns like other protein fibers. Silk is soluble in sodium hydroxide; however, it dissolves more slowly than wool.

USES

Silk is used primarily in apparel and home-furnishing items because of its appearance and cost. Silk is extremely versatile and can be used to create a variety of fabrics from sheer, gossamer chiffons to heavy, beautiful brocades and velvets. Because of silk's absorbency, it is appropriate for warm-weather wear. Because of its low heat conductivity, it is also appropriate for cold-weather wear. In furnishings, silk is often blended with other fibers to add a soft luster to the furnishing fabric. Silk blends are often used in window-treatment and upholstery fabrics. Occasionally, beautiful and expensive handmade rugs will be made of silk.

8

Introduction to Man-Made Fibers

In 1664, Robert Hooke suggested that if a proper liquid were squeezed through a small aperture and allowed to congeal, a fiber like that of the silkworm might be produced. In 1889, the first successful fiber was made from a solution of cellulose by a Frenchman, Count de Chardonnet. In 1910, rayon fibers were commercially produced in the United States, and acetate was produced in 1924. By 1939, the first noncellulosic, or synthetic, fiber—nylon—was made. Since that time, many more generic fibers and modifications or variants of these generic fibers have appeared on the market. The increasing number of new fiber names appearing on labels can create a great deal of confusion for the consumer.

Man-Made Fibers   Generic Names

Cellulosic	Noncellulosic or Synthetic		Mineral
Acetate	Acrylic	Nytril*	Glass
(Triacetate*)	Anidex*	Olefin	Metallic
Rayon	Aramid	PBI	
	Azlon*	Polyester	
	(Lastrile*)	Rubber	
	Modacrylic	Saran	
	Novoloid	Spandex	
	Nylon	Sulfar	
		Vinal*	
		Vinyon*	

*Not produced in the United States.

Legislation and Generic Names

In 1958, Congress passed legislation to regulate labeling of textiles in order to protect the consumer through the enforcement of ethical practices and to protect the producer from unfair competition resulting from the unrevealed presence of substitute materials in textile products. This law, the Textile Fiber Product Identification Law, covers *all* fibers except those already covered by the Wool Products Labeling Act, with certain other exceptions.

Although the law was passed in 1958, it did not become effective until 1960. During this interval, the Federal Trade Commission held hearings in regard to inequalities or injustices that the law might cause. Then it established rules and regulations to be observed in enforcing the law. The following list of man-made fiber generic names was established by the Federal Trade Commission in cooperation with the fiber producers. A *generic name* is the name of a family of fibers all having similar chemical composition. (Definitions of these generic names are included with the discussions of each fiber.)

The following information, in English, is required on the label for most textile items.

1. The percent of each natural or man-made fiber present must be listed in the order of predominance by weight. The percent listed must be correct within a tolerance of 3 percent. What that means is that if the label states a fiber content of 50 pecent cotton, the minimum can be no less than 47 percent and the maximum can be no more than 53 percent.

If a fiber or fibers represent less than 5 percent by weight, the fiber cannot be named unless it has a clearly established and definite functional significance. In those cases where the fiber has a definite function, the generic name, percentage by weight, and functional significance must be listed. For example, a garment that has a small amount of spandex, may have a label that reads "96% Nylon, 4% Spandex for elasticity."

2. The name of the manufacturer or the company's registered number such as WPL or RN. In many cases, the company's registered number is listed with the letters and the number. (Trademarks may serve as identification, but they are not required information. Often a trademark is listed with the generic fiber name.)

3. The first time a trademark appears in the required information, it must appear in immediate conjunction with the generic name and in type or lettering of equal size and conspicuousness. When the trademark is used elsewhere on the label, the generic name shall accompany it in legible and conspicuous type the first time it appears.

4. The name of the country where the product was processed or manufactured, such as "Made in USA." If the item was manufactured in the United States from imported fabric, the label might read "Made in USA of imported fabric."

Trade Names

An experimental fiber may be given a *trade name* (trademark), which distinguishes the fiber from other fibers of the same generic family that are made and sold by other producers. A producer may adopt a single trade name, word, or symbol, which may be used to cover all (or a large group) of the fibers made by that company. For example, "Orlon" is no longer used to designate a single acrylic fiber made by Du Pont, but is a broad descriptive name covering a family of related Du Pont acrylic fibers, each of which is sold to the manufacturer by type number. Trade names are also usually protected by a quality-control program.

The fiber producer must assume all the responsibility for promoting the fiber. The company must sell not only to its customers, the manufacturers, and retailers, but to the customer's customer—the consumer.

Fiber Spinning

It took many years to develop the first spinning solutions and devise spinnerets to convert the solutions into filaments. The first solutions were made by treating cellulose so it would dissolve in certain substances. It was not until the 1920s and 1930s that we first learned how to build long-chain molecules from simple substances.

All man-made fiber spinning processes are based on these three general steps.

1. Preparing a viscous or syrupy dope.

2. Extruding the dope through a spinneret to form a fiber.

3. Solidifying the fiber by coagulation, evaporation, or cooling.

The *raw material* may be a natural product such as cellulose or protein, or it may be chemicals that are synthesized into resins. These raw materials are made into solutions by dissolving them with chemicals or by melting. The solution is referred to as the *spinning solution,* or *dope.*

Extrusion is a very important part of the spinning process. It consists of forcing or pumping the spinning solution through the tiny holes of a spinneret.

A *spinneret* is a small thimble-like nozzle (Figure 8–1). Rayon is spun through a spinneret that is made of platinum—one of the few metals that will withstand the action of acids and alkalies. Acetate and other fibers are extruded through stainless-steel spinnerets. Spinnerets are costly—as much as $1,000 each—and new developments are closely guarded secrets. The making of the tiny holes is the critical part of the process. Fine hair-like instruments or laser beams are used. Ordinarily the holes are round, but many other shapes are used for special fiber types (see page 8).

Each hole in the spinneret forms one fiber. *Filament fibers* are spun from spinnerets with 350 holes or less. Together these fibers make a filament yarn. *Filament tow* is an untwisted rope of thousands of fibers. This rope is made by putting together the fibers from 100 or more spinnerets, each of which may have as many as three thousand holes (Figure 8–2). This large rope of fibers is crimped and is then ready to be made into staple by cutting to the desired length. (See Chapter 19 for methods of breaking filament tow into staple.)

Spinning Methods. Spinning is done by five different methods. These methods are compared briefly in Figure 8–3. Details of the methods are given in later chapters.

Man-made fibers are produced to satisfy a market or supply a special need. The first man-made fibers made it possible for the consumer to

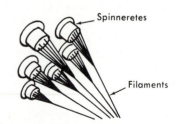

Fig. 8–1 Spinnerets. (Courtesy of AVTEX Fibers, Inc.)

Fiber from Several Spinnerets

Fig. 8–2 *Collecting fibers from several spinnerets to make a rope, called filament tow, which will be cut into staple fiber.*

grams correct any problems that arise and produce new fiber types modified for special end uses.

Common Fiber Modifications

One advantage of the man-made fibers is that each step of the production process can be precisely controlled to "tailor," or modify, the parent fiber. These modifications are the result of a producer's continuing research program to correct any limitations, explore the potential of its fibers, and develop properties that will give greater versatility in the end uses of the fibers.

The *parent fiber* is the fiber in its simplest form. It is often sold as a "commodity fiber" by generic name only, without benefit of a trade name. The parent fiber has been called by the following names: regular, basic, standard, conventional, or first-generation fiber.

Modifications of the parent fiber are usually sold under a brand or trade name. Modifications are also referred to as types, variants, or second-generation fibers.

The following are fiber modifications of the second generation:

1. Modification of fiber shape:
Cross-section, thick and thin, hollow

2. Modification of molecular structure and crystallinity:
High tenacity, low pilling, low elongation

3. Additives to polymer or fiber solution:
Cross dye, antistatic, sunlight resistance, fire retardant

4. Modifications of spinning procedures:
Crimp, fiberfill.

Complex modifications have been engineered to combine two polymers as separate entities within a single fiber or yarn. These have been referred to as third-generation fibers.

1. Bicomponent fibers
2. Blended filament yarns

have silk-like fabrics at low cost. The synthetics gave the consumer fabrics with improved properties unlike any natural fiber fabric.

The production program for a new fiber is long and expensive, and millions of dollars are invested before any profit can be realized. First, a research program is planned to develop the new fiber. Then a pilot plant is built to scale-up laboratory procedures to commercial production. This pilot plant may produce as much as 5 million pounds of fiber, which is used to test and evaluate the fiber and to determine and evaluate end uses. When the fiber is ready, a commercial plant is built.

A patent on the process gives the producer 17 years of exclusive right to the use of the process—time to recover the initial cost and make a profit. The price per pound during this time is high, but it drops later. The patent owner can license other producers to use the process. Continuing research and developmental pro-

Wet Spinning: Acrylic, Rayon, Spandex

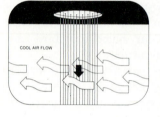

1. Raw material is dissolved by chemicals.
2. Fiber is spun into chemical bath.
3. Fiber solidifies when coagulated by bath.

Oldest process
Most complex
Weak fibers until dry
Washing, bleaching, etc., required before use

Dry Spinning:
Acetate, Acrylic, Modacrylic, Spandex, Triacetate, Vinyon

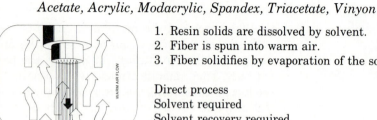

1. Resin solids are dissolved by solvent.
2. Fiber is spun into warm air.
3. Fiber solidifies by evaporation of the solvent.

Direct process
Solvent required
Solvent recovery required
No washing, etc., required

Melt Spinning: Nylon, Olefin, Polyester, Saran

1. Resin solids are melted in autoclave.
2. Fiber is spun out into the air.
3. Fiber solidifies on cooling.

Least expensive
Direct process
High spinning speeds
No solvent, washing, etc., required
Fibers shaped like spinneret hole

Dispersion or Emulsion Spinning: Polytetrafluoroethylene

1. Polymer is dispersed as fine particles in a carrier.
2. Dispersed polymer is extruded through a spinneret and coalesced by heating.
3. Carrier is removed by heating or dissolving.

Expensive
Used only for those fibers that are insoluble
Carrier required

Reaction Spinning: Spandex

1. Monomers are placed in solution.
2. Polymerization occurs during extrusion through spinneret system of reactants.
3. Solvents may be used to control fiber size.

Simple recovery of solvents
Less expensive than dry spinning for spandex
Difficult to get uniform, light fibers

Modification of Shape

NONROUND FIBER TYPES

Changing the cross-sectional shape is the easiest way to alter the mechanical and aesthetic properties of a fiber. This is usually done by changing the shape of the spinneret hole to produce the fiber shapes desired. All kinds of shapes are possible: flat, trilobal, quadralobal, pentalobal, triskelion, cruciform, clover leaf, and alphabet shapes such as Y and T (see page 8).

The *flat shape* was one of the first variations produced. "Crystal" acetate and "sparkling" nylon were ribbon-like fibers that were extruded through a long, narrow spinneret hole. Flat fibers tend to catch and reflect light much as a mirror does, so fabrics have a glint or sparkle. The *trilobal shape* has been widely used in both nylon and polyester fibers (Figure 8–4). It is spun through a spinneret with three triangularly arranged slits. The trade name Antron designates selected round, trilobal, and pentalobal fibers made by Du Pont. The following are some of the advantages of trilobal shape:

· Beautiful silk-like hand (depending on end-use requirements)
· Subtle opacity

· Soil-hiding (cloaks dirt)
· Built-in bulk without weight
· Moisture-heightened wicking action
· Silk-like sheen and color
· Crush resistance in heavy deniers
· Gives good textured crimp.

Cadon is a *triskelion*-shaped fiber (a three-sided configuration similar to a boat propeller) carpet nylon by Monsanto. Trevira® is a *pentalobal* polyester fiber produced by Hoechst (see Figure 8–5). Encron 8 is *octolobal*. "Touch" nylon has a *Y-shaped* cross-section. All these fibers have characteristics similar to the trilobal fibers. Dacron Type 83 is a *cruciform*-shaped staple fiber (shaped like a cross) with a crisper, more cotton-like hand. It has been optically whitened. It has been suggested that the cruciform shape might be the perfect shape for a fiber.

THICK-AND-THIN FIBER TYPES

Thick-and-thin fiber types have variations in diameter along their length as a result of uneven drawing or stretching after spinning. When woven into cloth, these yarns give the effect of a duppioni silk fabric or give a linen-like texture. The thick areas, or nubs, will dye a deeper color to create interesting tone-on-tone color effects. Barré in knits can be eliminated by thick-and-thin yarns. Many surface textures are possible by changing the size and length of the nubs or slubs.

Fig. 8–4 *Stereoscan photograph of trilobal nylon. (Courtesy of E. I. du Pont de Nemours & Company.)*

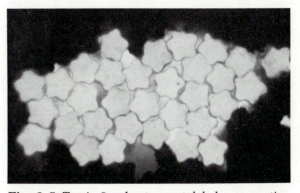

Fig. 8–5 *Trevira® polyester pentalobal cross-section 312×. (Courtesy of Hoechst Fibers Industries.)*

HOLLOW, OR MULTICELLULAR, FIBER TYPES

The hair or fur of many animals contains air cells that provide insulation in cold weather. The feathers of birds are hollow to give them buoyancy. Similar air cells and hollow filaments are possible in man-made fibers by the use of gas-forming compounds added to the spinning solution, by air injection at the jet face as the fiber is forming, or by the shape of the spinneret holes.

Hollow melt-spun fibers can be formed by pyrolizing a portion of the polymer flowing to the spinneret to form gas and then extruding the bubble containing polymer as hollow filaments. The spinneret hole can be shaped to produce hollow fibers. When extruded through a C-shaped hole, the fiber closes immediately. Other spinneret holes spin the fiber as two halves that immediately close to make the hollow fiber (see Figure 8–6). Examples of trade names of hollow fibers include Hollofil and Quallofil by du Pont.

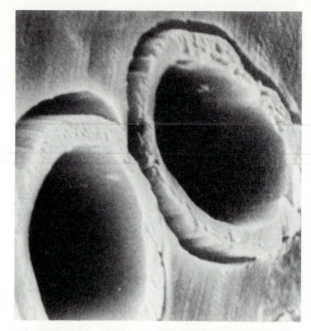

Fig. 8–6 Cross-section of Hollofil polyester. (Courtesy of E. I. du Pont de Nemours & Company.)

Modifications of Molecular Structure and Crystallinity

HIGH-TENACITY FIBER TYPES

Stretching a fiber changes its stress/strain curve, which is the basis of tenacity. Fiber strength is increased by (1) drawing or stretching the fiber to align or orient the molecules, thus strengthening the intermolecular forces, and/or by (2) chemical modification of the fiber polymer to increase the degree of polymerization.

High-tenacity rayon results from the rate of coagulation, the spinning speed, and/or modifiers added to the spinning solution. The spinning speed for *regular rayon* is quite high and the coagulation and regeneration occur almost simultaneously. This results in the formation of an oriented skin and amorphous core. In high-tenacity rayon, the spinning speed is reduced and the zinc sulfate content of the bath is increased, so there is an increase in the proportion of skin and a decrease in the core to the point

where the core may disappear and the fiber will be an all-skin structure. The increase in orientation of an all-skin fiber increases tensile strength. Stretching is done by passing the fibers around two Godet wheels, one of which rotates faster than the other. After the high-tenacity fiber emerges from the coagulating bath, it is then given a high degree of stretch in a hot-water or dilute-acid bath. This stretching increases orientation and strength. Figure 8–7 is a photomicrograph of a high-tenacity all-skin rayon. Amino compounds may be added to the spinning solution to increase the viscosity and produce a higher degree of polymerization.

High-strength rayons are suitable for blending with nylons and polyesters. They are widely used for industrial purposes such as in conveyor belts and tire cord. Comiso is a high-strength apparel fiber made by Beaunit. Tyrex, Dynacor, and Suprenka are trade names for tire cord.

High-Tenacity Synthetic Fibers. Molecular chain length can be varied in the melt-spun fibers at the polymer stage by changes in time, temperature, pressure, and chemicals. Long molecules are harder to pull apart than short molecules. Hot drawing of polyester and cold drawing of nylon align the molecules in such a way that the intermolecular forces are strengthened. Some of the high-tenacity (low-elongation)

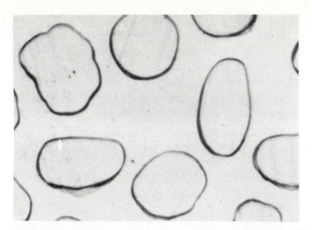

Fig. 8–7 *High-tenacity rayon fiber. (Courtesy of AVTEX Fibers, Inc.)*

nylons and polyesters were designed to strengthen cotton blends for durable press. Polyester's stress/strain curve more closely matches that of cotton, so they "pull together" to give greater durability.

High-tenacity polyester is now used in tire cord. Nylon has always had its widest use in industrial items such as tires for cars, trucks, and planes. Aramid fibers are the strongest and toughest fibers that have ever been made.

LOW-PILLING FIBER TYPES

Low-pilling fiber types are engineered to reduce the flex life by reducing the molecular weight as measured in terms of intrinsic viscosity. When flex-abrasion resistance is reduced, the fiber balls (pills) break off almost as soon as they are formed and the fabric retains its attractive appearance. These low-pilling fibers are not as strong as other types but are durable enough for apparel uses and are particularly suited to soft knitting yarns. (Review the discussion of molecular weight in Chapter 2.)

Dacron Type 35 is a higher-modulus, low-pilling staple fiber for blending with cotton. Type 65 is an extremely low-pilling, basic-dyeing staple for knitted garments; Dacron 107-W and Trevira Type 350 are optically brightened, pill-resistant staple for cotton/polyester blends in underwear.

BINDER STAPLE

Binder staple is a semidull, crimped polyester with a very low melting point. (Melting point relates to molecular structure.) It was designed to develop a thermoplastic bond with other fibers under heat and pressure. It sticks at 165°F and will shrink 55–75 percent at 200°F; Type 450 Fortrel is a fiber of this type.

LOW-ELONGATION FIBER TYPES

Low-elongation fiber types are designed as reinforcing fibers to increase the strength and abrasion resistance of cotton and cellulosic fabrics. The low elongation results from changing the balance of tenacity and extension. High-tenacity fibers have lower elongation properties. End uses are mainly in work clothing—items that get hard wear. Kodel 421 is a low-elongation fiber for use in blends with cotton.

Additives to the Polymer, or Spinning, Solution

DELUSTERING

The basic fiber is usually a *bright* fiber. It reflects light from its surface. To deluster a fiber, titanium dioxide—a white pigment—is added to the spinning solution before the fiber is extruded. In some cases, the titanium dioxide can be mixed in at an earlier stage, while the resin polymer is being formed. The degree of luster can be controlled by varying the amount of delusterant, producing dull or semidull fibers. Figure 8–8 shows three cones of yarn of different lusters.

Delustered fibers can be identified under the microscope by what appear to be peppery black spots (Figure 8–8). The particles of pigment absorb light or prevent reflection of light. Absorbed light causes degradation, or "tendering," of the fiber. For this reason, bright fibers that reflect light suffer less light damage and are better for use in curtains and draperies. The initial strength of a delustered fiber is less than that of a bright fiber. Rayon, for example, is 3–5 percent weaker when it is delustered.

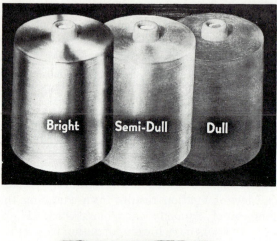

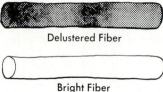

Delustered Fiber

Bright Fiber

Fig. 8–8 (Top) *Rayon yarns. (Courtesy of AVTEX Fibers, Inc.)* (Bottom) *Fibers as they would look under a microscope.*

SOLUTION DYEING OR MASS PIGMENTATION

Solution dyeing, or mass pigmentation, was developed in response to the gas-fading of many dyes used to dye acetate. *Solution dyeing* is the addition of colored pigments or dyes to the spinning solution. These fibers are referred to as *solution dyed, mass pigmented, dope dyed, spun dyed,* or *producer colored.* If the color is added before the fiber hardens, the term *gel dyeing* may be used. Solution dyeing offers the potential of providing color permanence that is not obtainable in any other way. The lightfastness and washfastness are unchanged for the life of the item. Because the color is uniformly distributed throughout the fiber, crocking and other color changes with use are not problems.

Because of the difficulty in obtaining a truly black dye that has reasonable colorfastness properties, black pigments are usually the first ones to be used. Other colors beyond black are produced as suitable colorfast pigments are developed. Solution-dyed fibers cost more per pound than uncolored fibers. This difference is offset later by the cost of yarn or piece (fabric) dyeing. The solution-dyed fibers are used in all kinds of end uses, such as upholstery, window-

treatment fabrics, and apparel. One disadvantage of the solution-dyed fibers is that the manufacturer must carry a large inventory to be able to fill orders quickly. The manufacturer is also less able to adjust to fashion changes in color, because it is not possible to strip color from these fibers and redye them.

WHITENERS AND BRIGHTENERS

Whiteners and *brighteners* are added to the spinning solution to make whiter fibers or fibers that resist yellowing. The additive used is an optical bleach or fluorescent dye that causes a whiter light to be reflected from the cloth. These whiteners are permanent to washing and dry cleaning. They are an advantage in many items because they eliminate the necessity for bleaching.

CROSS-DYEABLE FIBER TYPES

Cross-dyeable fiber types are very different from solution-dyed fibers. Solution-dyed fibers have colored pigment added to the spinning solution, so they are colored as they emerge from the spinneret.

Cross-dyeable fiber types are made by incorporating dye-accepting chemicals into the molecular structure. Some of the parent fibers are nondyeable or have poor acceptance of certain classes of dyes; the cross-dyeable types were developed to correct this limitation. Cross-dyeable types are white when spun, but will react with dyes later when the fabric is to be colored.

Two or more of these cross-dyeable fiber types can be used in a fabric that is then immersed in a suitable dye-bath mixture, and each fiber type reacts to pick up a different color. As many as five colors have been achieved in one dye bath. Designs may be heather, tone-on-tone, floral, or geometric, depending on the arrangement of the fiber types within the fabric. Solution-dyed fibers may be combined with cross-dyeable fiber types to increase color possibilities. Some of the cross-dyeable fiber types are basic dyeable, acid dyeable, disperse dyeable, acid-dye resist basic dyeable, and nondyeable.

ANTISTATIC FIBER TYPES

Static is a result of the flow of electrons. Fibers conduct electricity according to how readily electrons move in them. If static builds up in a fiber so that it has an excess of electrons, it is negatively charged and it will be attracted to something that is positively charged—something that has a deficiency of electrons. This attraction is illustrated by the way clothing clings to the body. Water will dissipate static. Because the heat-sensitive fibers, especially the synthetics, have such low water absorbency, static charges will build up rapidly during cold, dry weather, and they are slow to dissipate. If the fibers can be made wettable, the static charges will dissipate quickly and there will be no annoying static buildup.

For the person whose clothes are clinging, an immediate but temporary solution is that of using a wet sponge or paper towel and rubbing it over the garment or slip to drain away the static. The benefits will last much longer if one of the fabric softeners is used in place of plain water. Finishes and sprays are applied to the surface of the fiber and are lost during washing and wear.

The antistatic fiber types give durable protection because the fiber is made wettable by incorporating an antistatic compound—a chemical conductor—in the fiber so that it becomes an integral part of the fiber. The compound is added to the fiber-polymer raw material so that it is evenly distributed throughout the fiber-dope or spinning solution. It changes the fiber's hydrophobic nature to a hydrophilic one and raises the moisture regain so that static is dissipated more quickly. The moisture content of the air in the home should be kept high enough to provide moisture for absorption. Even "bone-dry" cotton will build up static. Static control is also achieved by incorporating a conductive fila-

Fig. 8–9 *Antistatic polyester. (Courtesy of E. I. du Pont de Nemours & Company.)*

ment into the filament (Figure 8–9). In the chart, Antistatic Fiber Variants, trade names and end uses are listed.

The soil-release benefits of the antistatic fiber types has been outstanding. The antistatic fibers retard soiling by minimizing the attraction and retention of dirt particles, and the opacity and luster in the yarn have soil-hiding properties. Soil redisposition in laundry is dramatically reduced. Oily stains, even motor oils, are released easily.

Antistatic Fiber Variants

Parent Fiber	Trademark	Fiber Modification	End Use	Producer
Nylon	Antron III	Three filaments of carbon-black core surrounded by sheath of nylon	Apparel Carpets	du Pont
Nylon	X-Stat	Seven silver-coated nylon filaments	Carpets	
Nylon	Ultron	Conjugate spun 95 percent nylon 6,6 and 5 percent nylon/carbon-black polymer stripe	Carpets	Monsanto
Nylon	Bodyfree		Apparel	Allied Chemical
Nylon	Enkalure	Fine denier–anticling	Apparel	American Enka
Polyester	Dacron III (Figure 8–9)	Polymeric conductive core	Carpets	du Pont

SUNLIGHT-RESISTANT TYPES

Ultraviolet light is the source of fiber degeneration as well as color fading. When ultraviolet light is absorbed, the damage results from an oxidation-reduction reaction between the radiant energy and the fiber or fiber dye. Stabilizers such as nitrogenous compounds may be added to the fiber to increase their light resistance. These stabilizers must be carefully selected for the fiber and the dye. Estron SLR is a sunlight-resistant acetate fiber. Delustered fibers are more sensitive to sunlight than bright fibers.

FLAME-RESISTANT FIBER TYPES

Flame-resistant fiber types give better protection to consumers than do topical flame-retardant finishes (see Chapter 35).

The man-made fibers that are always flame resistant are aramid, novolid, modacrylic, glass, PBI, saran, sulfar, and vinyon. Other man-made fibers can be modified by changing their polymer structure or by adding water-insoluble compounds to the spinning solution. These fiber modifications make the fibers inherently flame resistant. The fibers vary in their resistance to flame.

The following chart lists the naturally fire-resistant fibers produced in the United States.

Modifications of Spinning Procedure

When producers started to make staple fiber, mechanical crimping was done to broken filaments and later to filament tow to make the fibers more cohesive and thus easier to spin into yarns. Other techniques were developed to give permanent crimp to rayon and acetate and to provide bulk or stretch to all fibers—filaments as well as staple.

Crimping of fibers is important in many end uses for cover and loft in bulky knits, blankets, carpets, battings for quilted items, pillows, and the like, and for stretch and economy in hosiery and sportswear. One of the first crimping techniques was developed for use with rayon.

Viscose rayon fiber with latent or potential crimp is produced by coagulating the fiber in a bath of lower acid and higher salt concentration. A skin forms around the fiber and then bursts. A thinner skin forms over the rupture. The crimp develops when the fiber is immersed in water. Avicron is a latent-crimp rayon fiber made by American Viscose. It is a heavy-denier novelty filament fiber used in pile fabrics (Figures 8–10 and 8–11).

Crimped polyester fibers are used for fiberfill

Flame-Resistant Fibers*

Fiber Name	Trade Name	Producer
Aramid	Kevlar, Nomex	E. I. du Pont de Nemours
Glass	Star Rov, Stran Vitron, Vitron-Strand	Manville Corp.
Glass	Fiberglas Beta	Owens-Corning Fiberglas Corp.
Glass	LEX, TEXO	PPG Industries, Inc.
Modacrylic	SEF	Monsanto Chemicals Co., Fibers Div.
PBI	Arazole	Celion Carbon Fibers
Saran		Ametek, Inc.
Sulfar		Albany International
Sulfar		Johnson Filament
Sulfar	Ryton	Phillips Fiber Corp.
Sulfar	PPS	Shakespere Monofilament

Textile World, August, 1986.

Fig. 8–10 *Cross-section of Avicron rayon. Note the difference in thickness of the skin on the two sides. (Courtesy of AVTEX Fibers, Inc.)*

batting for pillows, furniture, carpets, sleeping bags, and quilted apparel. The fiberfill used for furniture is made into bats that are needle-punched to prevent lumping. Helically (spiral) crimped fibers are produced by cooling one side of the fiber faster than the other side as the melt-spun fiber is extruded. This uneven cooling causes a curl to form in the fiber. The same effect

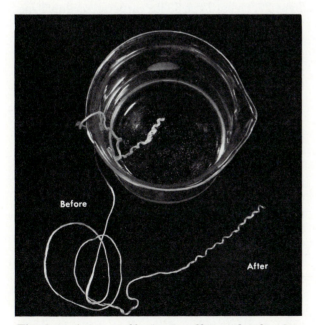

Fig. 8–11 *Avicron self-crimping fiber curls when immersed in water.*

can be achieved by heating one side of the fiber during the stretching or drawing process. This helical crimp has more springiness than the conventional mechanical sawtooth crimp, and these fibers are used where high levels of compressional resistance and recovery are needed.

Bulky yarns were developed by throwsters to make stretch fabrics about 1950 (see Chapter 18). In the 1970s, fiber producers started texturizing yarns. Undrawn and partially drawn yarns are sold for texturizing.

Third-Generation Fiber Types

BICOMPONENT FIBERS

A *bicomponent fiber* is a fiber consisting of two polymers that are chemically different, physically different, or both. If the two components would fall into two different generic classes, the term *bicomponent bigeneric* may be used. Bicomponent fibers may be of several types. In the first type, the fibers are spun with the two polymers side-by-side, called *bilateral*. In the second type, one polymer is surrounded by another in an arrangement called a *core sheath*. In the third type, short fibrils of one polymer are imbedded in another polymer called a *matrix fibril* (see Figure 8–12).

The original discovery that the two sides of a fiber can react differently when wet was made during studies of wool in 1886. In 1953, it was discovered that the difference in reaction was the result of the bicomponent nature of wool, which results from a difference in growth rate and in chemical composition. To produce a bicomponent rayon, two viscose solutions—one aged and one unaged—are spun through spinneret holes, each of which is separated into two halves by a divider through the center (Figure 8–12). The resulting fiber has a side-by-side, or bilateral, arrangement. This fiber is straight as it is spun but will crimp when immersed in hot or cold water and will retain its crimp after it dries. Crimp potential of this kind is referred to as *latent*, or *inherent, crimp*. When the latent crimp of a bicomponent, bilateral fiber is devel-

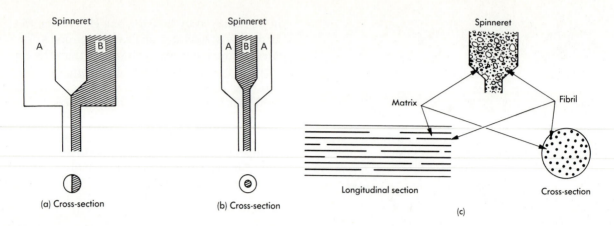

(a) Cross-section   (b) Cross-section   (c)

Longitudinal section   Cross-section

Matrix   Fibril

Fig. 8–12 Bicomponent fiber structure: (a) bilateral; (b) core-sheath; (c) matrix-fibril.

oped by heat and/or moisture, it is a three-dimensional helical crimp with the shorter component on the inside. Helical crimp (or curl) gives more bulk and stretch than other types of crimp.

The pipe-in-pipe procedure is another way to spin bicomponent fibers. In this case a sheath-core structure is formed, one component forming the sheath and the other the core (Figure 8–12).

Conjugate spinning was used in 1959 to produce Orlon 21 (Figure 8–13), the first acrylic bicomponent bilateral structure that would respond to wetting and drying in the same manner as the wool fiber. The fiber is spun straight and made into a garment such as a sweater, which is then exposed to heat; one side of the fiber shrinks and the fiber takes on a helical crimp. The reaction of the fibers to water occurs during laundering. As the fiber gets wet, one side swells and the fiber uncrimps. As the crimp relaxes, the sweater increases in size. The crimp will return as the sweater dries and it will regain its

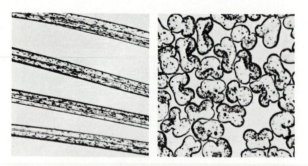

Fig. 8–13 Photomicrographs of semidull Orlon Sayelle: longitudinal (left) *and cross-sectional* (right) *views. (Courtesy of E. I. du Pont de Nemours & Company.)*

original size if properly handled. The sweater should not be drip-dried or placed on a towel to dry because the weight of the water and the resistance of the towel will prevent the sweater from regaining its original size. The right way to dry the sweater is to either machine dry it at low temperatures or place it on a smooth, flat surface and "bunch-it-in" to help the crimp recover. This Orlon bicomponent fiber is called a *reversible crimp fiber* because of the uncrimping and crimp recovery action during the laundry process. When Orlon 21 is used in quality products, the trade name Sayelle is used on the label.

Other bicomponent acrylic fibers are Orlon Type 27, Orlon Type 33 for carpets, Acrilan Type 45 for carpets, Creslan Type 68-B, and Creslan Type 83 CF-5 carpet fiber. Civona is a bicomponent Orlon that was created for worsted spun-machine knitting yarns having a fine, Merino wool–like handle. Bi-loft is a bicomponent acrylic made by Monsanto for apparel.

The bicomponent fibers have been classified as latent-crimp-water (viscose) and latent-crimp-heat types. Nylon bicomponents are of the latter type. Nylon was the first of the synthetics to be made as a bicomponent fiber. Cantrece was the trade name adopted by du Pont for hosiery made of its monofilament-bicomponent fiber. Cantrece I was introduced in 1963, but it lacked the elastic recovery needed to prevent bagging at the knees. After a period of research, Cantrece II was introduced successfully. Like the other synthetic bicomponent fibers (Types 880, 881, 882, and 890 are used in Cantrece products), the two sides of the fiber differ in their reaction to heat. One side will shrink, causing the fiber to curl helically.

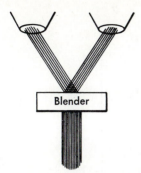

Fig. 8–14 *Blended filament yarn. Different fibers are spun, then blended to form a yarn.*

Bicomponent polyester and olefin fibers have been developed for use in the clothing, upholstery, and carpet fields. Cordelan is a vinal/vinyon bicomponent-bigeneric flame-resistant fiber. It is made of three polymers: polyvinyl chloride, polyvinyl alcohol, and a copolymer of PVC/PVA. It is a matrix fibril–type fiber.

BLENDED FILAMENT YARNS

Blended filament yarn differs from bicomponent and bicomponent-bigeneric fibers in that the blending takes place after the fibers are spun (Figure 8–14). This is a less-complex combination and can be made from a wider range of materials; the combinations can be tested very quickly in fabric form.

Lanese is Celanese's trademark for its acetate/polyester core-bulked filament yarn used in apparel and home-furnishing fabrics (Figure 8–15). Creslan 67A, 67AB, and 710 are blends

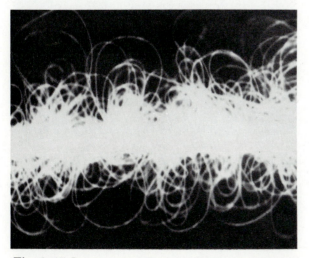

Fig. 8–15 *Lanese yarn. (Courtesy of Celanese Fibers, Inc.)*

of monocomponent and bicomponent Creslan acrylic staple fibers. SEF modacrylic types SX6 and SX7 are producer blends of 65 percent SEF modacrylic and Spectran polyester.

ROTOFIL, OR FACIATED, YARNS

The purpose of these yarns is to give better texture and hand to fabrics. The yarns are combinations of coarse filaments for strength and fine broken filaments for softness. They are made by a combination of crimping and twisting. Trevira Dawn by Hoechst Fibers Industries is a polyester rotofil yarn.

Carpet Fibers

Carpeting is an end use in which a large volume of fiber or yarn is needed. Carpeting also requires a specific combination of fiber properties for satisfactory appearance and performance. The ideal carpet is durable, resilient (shows no traffic pattern), resistant to soil, and is easily cleaned. The major portion of a carpet consists of the fiber that forms the face. Fibers with high abrasion resistance make the most durable carpets, but the useful life of the carpet is also dependent on appearance retention—shedding, fading, "walked-down" areas, pilling, and soil and static resistance. Some carpets may need to be replaced before they are worn out. Wool was, at one time, the standard carpet fiber; but the amount of carpet wool produced throughout the world has declined, whereas the need for carpet fiber has increased tremendously. At present, nylon is the most widely used carpet fiber.

Abrasion Resistance. Abrasion resistance is the major factor in wear performance or durability. Durability has been defined as the time required to wear out the face fibers. The thickness of the yarn tufts, the denseness of the pile, and the kind of fiber are major factors in durability. In resistance to abrasion, the carpet fibers are rated as follows: nylon (unexcelled); polyester and olefins (very good); acrylics, modacrylics, and wool (good).

Comparison of Wool and Man-Made Carpet Fibers

Fiber Characteristic	Wool	Man-Made
Fiber diameter	Coarse–blends of various wools	15–18 denier or blend of various deniers
Fiber length	Staple	Staple or filament blend of various lengths
Crimp	3D Crimp	Sawtooth crimp, 3D crimp, bicomponent, textured filament
Cross-section	Oval	Round, trilobal, multilobal, square with voids, 5 pointed star
Resiliency and resistance to crushing	Good	Medium to excellent depending on fiber
Resistance to abrasion	Good	Good to excellent
Resistance to water-borne stains	Poor	Good to excellent
Resistance to oily stains	Good	Poor
Fire retardancy	Good	Modified fiber or topical finish
Static resistance	Good	Poor to good depending on fiber

Compressional Resiliency. Compressional resiliency is the tendency of a carpet fiber to spring back to its original height after being bent or otherwise deformed. This is particularly important in areas of heavy traffic or under the crushing force of the legs of heavy furniture. Nylon is unexcelled in overall recovery. Wool and the acrylics and polyesters are very satisfactory and have better immediate recovery. The cellulose fibers have poor recovery. As finer denier fibers were used to achieve a softer hand in the late 1970s, the autoclave heat setting process was developed so that these finer yarns performed with comparable resiliency.

Carpet fibers are larger in diameter than apparel fibers. This larger size gives the fiber more resistance to bending or crushing. A combination of different deniers is often used in a carpet.

Soiling. Soiling is a strongly fiber-dependent property. It may be real or "apparent." Soil retention is a function of fiber cross-sectional shape. "Apparent" soiling is a function of fiber color and optical properties, such as transparency or opacity, as well as fiber shape. Smooth circular fibers retain the minimum quantity of soil. However, when circular fibers are transparent, as nylon is, the soil shows through and the circular shape tends to magnify it, so the "apparent" soil seems much worse.

Fibers can be made more opaque by changing the cross-sectional shape from circular to nonround. Light is reflected by the angles of the indented surfaces of nonround fibers, giving them greater opacity. For this reason (as well as bulk), the trilobal and Y-shaped fibers are often used (Figure 8–16). However, in areas of heavy,

Fig. 8–16 *Trilobal carpet fiber. (Courtesy of E. I. du Pont de Nemours & Company.)*

oily soil, circular fibers may be better, as they have fewer crevices where soil can be deposited and from which it must be removed. The delustering agent, titanium dioxide, will increase the opacity of a fiber and thus reduce the apparent soiling, but it makes the carpet look dull and chalky and it affects dyeing properties. Nylon fibers have now been spun in such a way as to leave voids in the fiber that scatter light, thus giving the same effect as the delusterant (Figure 8–17). Fibers such as Stainmaster by du Pont can be modified to be soil resistant.

Static. Static is one of the annoying problems associated with carpets in terms of comfort (static shock) and soiling. Some fibers generate more static than others. Cut pile generates more static than loop pile. Some carpet backings are better conductors than others. Conductive carbon black can be added to the latex adhesive to reduce carpet static. The shoes worn by the individual have an effect on the amount of static produced. Shoes with leather soles and rubber heels generate more static than others.

Metallic fibers can be used in a limited way to control static. Brunsmet, a stainless steel fiber from 2 to 3 inches long, can be mixed throughout any kind of spun yarn to make the yarn a good conductor. Only one or two fibers per tuft will carry the static from the face fiber to the backing. So far, this kind of carpet yarn

U.S. Man-Made Fiber Capacity in Millions of Pounds in 1985*

Acetate and rayon	558
Acrylic	631
Glass	1394[1]
Nylon	2343
Olefin	1249
Polyester	3341

*Source: *Chemical and Engineering News,* June 9, 1986, page 38.
[1]Figure from 1984; 1985 information was not available.

has been used in places in which static is a special problem, such as hospitals and rooms where sensitive computer equipment is kept. Zefstat, an acrylic or nylon spun yarn by Badische, contains an especially treated strip of aluminum blended in so that it is invisible. As little as 2 percent aluminum will dissipate static as fast as it is generated. In addition, synthetic and man-made fibers can be modified to be antistatic, as explained earlier in the chapter.

***
Man-Made Fiber Capacity
***

In 1928, man-made fibers accounted for 5 percent of textile-fiber consumption in the United States; in 1986, man-made fibers comprise approximately 75 percent of U.S. textile consumption. See Figure 8–18, which compares domestic consumption of man-made fiber, cotton, and wool.

***
Man-Made versus Natural Fibers
***

Fig. 8–17 *Nylon fiber with voids. (Courtesy of E. I. du Pont de Nemours & Company.)*

A comparison of natural and man-made fibers is made in the following chart (page 80).

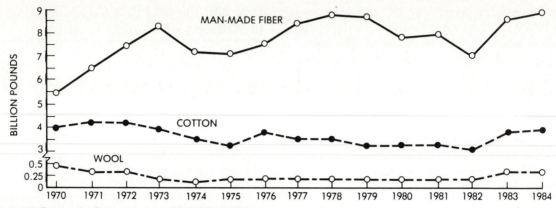

Fig. 8–18 *Domestic Consumption: Man-Made Fiber, Cotton, and Wool. (Courtesy of* Textile Organon, *March, 1985.)*

Comparison of Natural and Man-Made Fibers

Natural	Man-Made
Produced seasonally and stored until used	Continuous production
Vary in quality because they are affected by weather, nutrients, insects, or disease	Uniform in quality
Lack uniformity	Uniform or made purposely nonuniform
Physical structure depends on natural growth of plant or animal	Physical structure depends on fiber-spinning processes and after treatments
Chemical composition and molecular structure depend on natural growth	Chemical composition and molecular structure depend on starting materials
Properties are inherent	Properties are inherent
Properties conferred on fabrics can be changed by yarn and fabric finishes	Properties of fibers can be changed by varying spinning solutions and spinning conditions
	Properties conferred on fabrics can be changed by fabric finishes
Only silk is available in filament	Fibers can be any length
Less versatile	Versatile, changes can be made more quickly
Fibers are absorbent	Most (rayon and acetate are exceptions) have low absorbency
Not heat sensitive	Most (rayon is the exception) are heat sensitive)
Require fabric finish to be heat-set	Most (rayon and acetate are exceptions) can be heat-set
Research, development, and promotion done by trade organizations	Research, development, and promotion done by individual companies as well as by trade organizations

9

Rayon: A Man-Made Cellulosic Fiber

Rayon is a man-made cellulosic fiber in which the starting material, wood pulp or cotton linters, is physically changed. Rayon, the first man-made fiber, was developed before scientists knew much about molecular chains—how they are built up in nature or how they can be built up in the laboratory. The developers of rayon were trying to make artificial silk. Three methods of manufacturing rayon were developed in Europe in the 1880s and 1890s.

Frederick Schoenbein discovered in 1846 that cellulose would dissolve in a mixture of ether and alcohol if it were first treated with nitric acid, but the resulting fiber was highly explosive.

In 1884, Count Hilaire de Chardonnet, in France, made the first successful rayon by changing the nitrocellulosic fiber back to cellulose. This process was dangerous and difficult, and the nitrocellulosic process has not been used anywhere in the world since 1949.

In 1890, Louis Despeissis discovered that cellulose would dissolve in a cuprammonium solution, and in 1919 J. P. Bemberg made a commercially successful cuprammonium rayon. It was produced in the United States from 1926 until 1976. In 1892 in England, Cross, Bevan, and Beadle developed the viscose method. The viscose method is the only process currently used in the United States.

Commercial production of viscose rayon in the United States started in 1911 by the American Viscose Co. (Avtex Fibers). The fiber was sold as artificial silk until the name "rayon" was adopted in 1924. Viscose filament fiber, the first form of the fiber to be made, was a very bright, lustrous fiber. Because it had low strength, this fiber was used in the crosswise direction of the cloth; the lengthwise yarns were of silk, a fiber strong enough to withstand the tension of the loom. The double Godet wheel, invented in 1926, stretched the filaments and gave them strength. Delustering agents, which were added to the spinning solution, made it possible to have dull as well as bright fibers. Solution-dyed fibers came later.

In 1932, machinery was designed especially for making staple fiber. Large spinnerets with ten times as many holes were used and the fibers from several spinnerets were collected as a rope called *tow,* which was then crimped and cut.

The first uses of rayon were in crepe and linen-like apparel fabrics. The high twist that was required to make the crepe yarn reduced the bright luster of the fibers. "Transparent velvet" (made in France), sharkskin, tweed, challis, and chiffon were other fabrics made from these first rayons.

The physical properties of rayon remained about the same until 1940, when high-tenacity rayon for tires was developed. It proved to be superior to cotton for that use, and by 1957 cotton had disappeared from the tire-cord market. After high-tenacity tire cord and heavy-denier carpet fiber were developed, 65 percent of the rayon produced went into industrial and home-furnishing uses and less went into apparel.

Continued research and development led to what has been considered the greatest technological breakthrough in rayon—high-wet-modulus rayon. Production in the United States started in 1955. This modified fiber made it possible for rayon to be used for washable fabrics, dresses, sheets, towels, and also in blends with cotton. High-wet-modulus rayon stimulated a resurgence in the use of rayon in apparel.

High-wet-modulus rayon is frequently referred to as HWM rayon to distinguish it from regular or viscose rayon. In fact, HWM rayon is a viscose rayon, but in common usage viscose rayon refers to the weaker fiber. HWM rayon is also called high-performance (HP) rayon, or polynosic rayon. Polynosic has recently been adopted as a trade name by a U.S. company—this adds to the confusion of names because polynosic is used as a generic name for HWM rayon in Europe.

In 1960, 12 companies were producing rayon in the United States; in 1982, there were four producers, only one of which produced filament rayon.

Major producers of rayon in the United States include Avtex Fibers, Inc., BASF Corporation, Courtaulds North American, Inc., and North American Rayon Corporation. It is estimated that the output of rayon will not be increased because of the high cost of replacement machinery. Rayon is no longer the inexpensive fiber it once was—now it is generally comparable in price to cotton.

PRODUCTION

In the production of rayon, purified cellulose is chemically converted to a viscous solution that is pumped through spinnerets into a bath that

Spinning Processes for Viscose Rayon

Regular or Standard		High Wet Modulus
1. Blotter-like sheets of purified cellulose		1. Blotter-like sheets of purified cellulose
2. Steeped in caustic soda		2. Steeped in weaker caustic soda
3. Liquid squeezed out by rollers		3. Liquid squeezed out by rollers
4. Shredder crumbles sheets to alkali crumbs		4. Shredder crumbles sheets to alkali crumbs
5. Crumbs aged 50 hours		5. No aging
6. Crumbs treated with carbon disulfide to form cellulose xanthate, 32 percent CS_2		6. Crumbs treated with carbon disulfide to form cellulose xanthate, 39–50 percent CS_2
7. Crumbs mixed with caustic soda to form viscose solution		7. Crumbs mixed with 2.8 percent sodium hydroxide to form viscose solution
8. Solution aged 4–5 days		8. No aging
9. Solution filtered		9. Solution filtered
10. Pumped to spinneret and extruded into sulfuric acid bath		10. Pumped to spinneret and extruded into acid bath
10 percent H_2SO_4 16–24 percent Na_2SO_4 1–2 percent $ZnSO_4$	Spinning bath	1 percent H_2SO_4 4–6 percent Na_2SO_4
120 meters/minute	Spinning speed	20–30 meters/minute
45–50°C	Spinning-bath temperature	25–35°C
25 percent	Filaments stretched	150–600 percent

changes it back to solid 100 percent cellulose filaments. This is done by the wet-spinning process (see page 68). In the following chart, the processes for making regular and high-wet-modulus rayon are described. The differences in the spinning process produce fibers with different properties. In the high-wet-modulus process, the maximum chain length and fibril structure are maintained as much as possible.

A 1984 article in a technical journal stated that experiments were being made with solvent spinning of rayon. It was expected to go into commercial production by 1989 for industrial end uses.

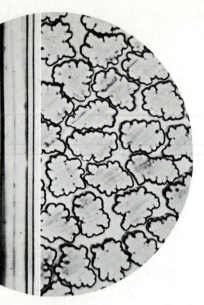

Fig. 9–1 *Photomicrographs of viscose rayon: longitudinal* (left) *and cross-sectional* (right) *views. (Courtesy of E. I. du Pont de Nemours & Company.)*

PHYSICAL STRUCTURE

Regular viscose is characterized by lengthwise lines called *striations*. The cross-section is a *serrated* circular shape (Figure 9–1). The shape of the fiber results from the presence of zinc sulfate in the spinning bath and from the liquid lost from the fiber during coagulation. The indented shape is an advantage in dye absorption because of an increase in surface area.

High-wet-modulus rayon that is spun into a bath with less zinc sulfate has a rounder cross-section. Figure 9–2 shows the difference in cross-sectional shapes of regular and high-wet-modulus rayon.

Filament rayon yarns have from 80–980 filaments per yarn and vary from 40–5,000 denier. Staple fibers and tow have a range of 1.5–15 denier, the 15 denier being carpet fiber or a heavy-use fiber. Staple fibers are usually crimped mechanically or by chemical means (Figure 9–3).

Rayon fibers are naturally very bright. This was one of the limitations to the use of the early fibers because bright filaments make very lustrous fabrics that are limited in use to dressy or luxury-type garments. The addition of delustering pigments (see page 71) remedied this problem. Pigment colors can be added to the fiber-spinning solution to make dull or colored fibers.

CHEMICAL COMPOSITION AND MOLECULAR STRUCTURE

Rayon—a manufactured fiber composed of regenerated cellulose, as well as manufactured fibers composed of regenerated cellulose in which substituents have replaced not more than 15 percent of the hydrogens of the hydroxyl groups.— Federal Trade Commission.

Rayon is 100 percent cellulose and has the same chemical composition as natural cellulose. The molecular structure of rayon is also the same as cotton and flax except that the rayon molecular chains are shorter and are not as crystalline. The breakdown of the cellulose occurs when the alkali cellulose and the viscose solution are aged. In regular rayon, the breakdown of the chains is quite severe. When the solution is spun into the acid bath, regeneration and coagulation

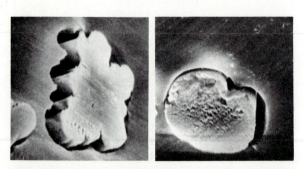

Fig. 9–2 *Stereoscan photograph of Fibro, regular rayon* (left) *and Vincel, high-wet-modulus rayon* (right). *(Courtesy of* Modern Textiles *magazine.)*

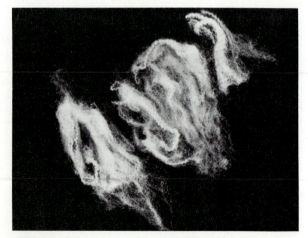

Fig. 9–3 *Crimp in viscose rayon staple.*

Comparison of Cotton, Regular Rayon, and High-Wet-Modulus Rayon

Properties	Cotton	Regular Rayon	High-Wet-Modulus Rayon
Fibrils	Yes	No	Yes
Molecular chain length	10,000	300–450	450–750
Swelling in water, percent	6	26	18
Average stiffness	57–60	6–50	28–75
Tenacity, grams/denier			
Dry	4.0	2.0	4.5
Wet	5.0	1.0	3.0
Breaking elongation, percent	12	11	30

take place very rapidly. Stretching aligns the molecules to give strength to the filaments.

In high-wet-modulus rayon, since the aging is eliminated, the molecular chains are not shortened as much. Because the acid bath is less concentrated, there is slower regeneration and coagulation so that more stretch and thus more orientation of the molecules can be made. HWM rayon retains its microfibrilar structure. This means its performance is more similar to cotton than to that of regular rayon. The following comparison chart shows the similarity between cotton and HWM rayon.

PROPERTIES

Rayon fibers are highly absorbent, soft, comfortable, easy to dye, and versatile. Fabrics made of these fibers have good drapability. Rayon fibers are used in apparel, home furnishings, medical/surgical products, and nonwovens.

Aesthetic. Since the luster, fiber length, and diameter of the fiber can be controlled, rayon can be made into cotton-like, linen-like, wool-like, and silk-like fabrics. As a blending fiber, rayon can be given much the same physical characteristics as the other fiber in the blend. If it is chosen instead of cotton or to blend with cotton, rayon can give the look of mercerized long-staple cotton to a fabric.

Durability. Regular rayon is not a very strong fiber and it loses about 50 percent of its strength when wet. The breaking tenacity is 0.7–2.6 g/d. Rayon has a breaking elongation of 15 percent dry and 20 percent wet and has the lowest elastic recovery of any fiber. All of these factors are the result of the amorphous regions in the fiber. Water enters the amorphous areas very readily,

Summary of the Performance of Rayon in Apparel Fabrics

	Regular Rayon	HWM Rayon
AESTHETIC	VARIABLE	VARIABLE
DURABILITY	LOW	MODERATE
Abrasion resistance	Low	Moderate
Tenacity	Low	Moderate
Elongation	Moderate	Low
COMFORT	EXCELLENT	EXCELLENT
Absorbency	High	Excellent
Thermal retention	Low	Low
APPEARANCE RETENTION	LOW	MODERATE
Resiliency	Low	Low
Dimensional stability	Low	Moderate
Elastic recovery	Low	Moderate
RECOMMENDED CARE	DRY CLEAN	MACHINE WASH

causing the molecular chains to separate as the fiber swells. This breaks the hydrogen bonds and permits distortion of the chains. When water is removed, new hydrogen bonds form, but in the distorted state.

HWM rayon has a more-crystalline and oriented structure so that the dry fiber is relatively strong. It has a breaking tenacity of 2.5–5.5 g/d, a breaking elongation of 6.5 percent dry and 7 percent wet, and an elastic recovery that is greater than that of cotton.

Comfort. Both types of rayon make very comfortable fabrics. They are absorbent, having a moisture regain of 13 percent. This eliminates any static. They are smooth and soft.

Appearance Retention. The resiliency of both rayons is low. This can be improved in HWM rayon fabrics by adding a durable-press finish. However, the finish may decrease strength and abrasion resistance. Dimensional stability of regular rayon is low. Fabrics may shrink or stretch. The fiber is very weak when wet and has low elastic recovery. Performance of HWM rayon is better—it exhibits moderate dimensional stability that can be improved by shrinkage-control finishes. The fiber is not likely to stretch out of shape and elastic recovery is moderate.

Care. Regular rayon fabrics have limited washability because of the low strength of the fibers when wet (0.7–1.8 g/d). Unless resin-treated, rayon fabrics have a tendency to shrink progressively. This shrinkage cannot be controlled by Sanforization. Regular rayon fabrics generally should be dry cleaned.

HWM rayon fabrics have greater washability. (Wet breaking tenacity of 1.8–4.0 g/d.) They have stability equal to cotton and strength equal to or better than cotton; they can be mercerized and Sanforized, and they wrinkle less than regular rayon in washing and drying.

The chemical properties of rayon are like those of cotton and other cellulosic fibers. They are harmed by acids, resistant to dilute alkalis, and are not affected by organic solvents; thus they can be safely dry cleaned. Rayon is attacked by silverfish and mildew.

Rayon is not greatly harmed by sunlight. It is not thermoplastic and thus can withstand a fairly high temperature for pressing. Rayon burns readily, like cotton.

USES

Rayon is the sixth most important fiber in the United States. Quantities produced have been decreasing; 607 million pounds in 1970, 461 million pounds in 1981, and 355 million pounds in 1982. Filament rayon has been decreasing in importance.

Uses of Rayon in 1984	Million Pounds
Woven fabrics	177.7
Nonwovens	126.3
Other uses	18.8
Circular and flat knits	4.3
Flocking	2.7
Carpet-face yarns	0.3
	331.8

Presently, rayon is mostly used in woven fabrics. In 1986, more rayon was seen in apparel, in both all-rayon fabrics as well as in blends with other fibers. Antique-satin drapery fabrics in a blend of rayon and acetate continue to be a classic fabric in interior decoration.

The second most important use of rayon is in nonwoven fabrics, where absorbency is important. Items include industrial wipes; medical supplies, including bandages; diapers; sanitary napkins; and tampons. These disposable products are biodegradable.

TYPES AND KINDS

Over the years, the uses of rayon have changed. Technology has developed so rapidly that, of the 160 types of rayon made now, only five of those types were made in 1976!

Types and Kinds of Rayon

Rayon	Trademark	Producer	Uses
Staple fiber	Fibro	Courtaulds	Apparel and home
	Fibrenka	BASF	furnishings
Filament, staple, tow	Narco	North American Rayon	Apparel and home
	Avtex Rayon	Avtex	furnishings
Solution dyed	Coloray	Courtaulds	Home furnishings and
	Jetspun	BASF	industrial
	Kolorbon	BASF	
	Skybloom	BASF	
Acid dyeable	Enkrome	BASF	Apparel and home
	Fibro DD	Courtaulds	furnishings
Varied cross-section	Enkaire	BASF	Apparel
	Viloft	Courtaulds	
Intermediate or high tenacity	Hi-Narco	North American Rayon	Industrial
	Super-Narco	North American Rayon	
	I. T.	BASF	
	Aviloc (adhesive treated)	Avtex	
	Fibro HT	Courtaulds	
High wet modulus	Avril	Avtex	Apparel and home
	Avril II	Avtex	furnishings
	Avril III	Avtex	
	Avril Prima	Avtex	
	Polynosic	BASF	
	Vincel	Courtaulds	
	Zantrel	BASF	
Optically brightened	Super White	BASF	All
Flame retardant	Durvil	Avtex	Apparel
High absorbency	Absorbit	BASF	Sanitary supplies
	Avsorb	Avtex	Sanitary supplies
Adhesive-treated yarns	Beau-grip	North American Rayon	Industrial
Rayon/cotton	Cotron	Avtex	All
Hollow filament	ViLoft		
Self-crimping	Avicron	American Viscose	Home furnishings

10

Acetate: The First Heat-Sensitive Fiber

Acetate was the second man-made fiber produced in the United States: production began in 1924. Acetate originated in Europe, using a technique to produce a spinning solution for a silk-like fiber. The early experiments were not successful because the treated cellulose was only soluble in an expensive, highly toxic solvent. It was later discovered that, with further treatment, a non-toxic, less-expensive solvent could be used. The Dreyfus brothers, who were experimenting with acetate in Switzerland, went to England during World War I and perfected the acetate "dope" as a varnish for airplane wings. After the war, they perfected the process of making acetate fibers.

More problems had to be solved with the acetate process than with the rayon processes, in which, unlike the acetate process, the treated cellulose was changed back to 100 percent cellulose. The acetate fiber is a different chemical compound. In the original acetate or primary acetate there were no hydroxyl groups; in the modified or secondary acetate there were only a few hydroxyl groups. Secondary acetate is usually referred to as acetate to distinguish it from triacetate, which has essentially no hydroxyl groups. Thus the fibers could not be dyed with any existing dyes. Disperse dyes were developed especially for acetate and triacetate.

Acetate had better properties than rayon for use in silk-like fabrics. It had natural body, which made it good for blends with rayon in staple form for wool-like fabrics.

When a new fiber comes on the market, problems often arise. Because acetate was the first thermoplastic or heat-sensitive fiber, consumers were confronted with fabrics that melted under a hot iron. This was a long time before durable-press fabrics and homemakers were accustomed to ironing all apparel. The problem was further confused because manufacturers introduced and named acetate as a kind of rayon.

Another problem with acetate was fume fading—a condition in which certain disperse dyes changed color (blue to pink, green to brown, gray to pink) as a result of atmospheric fumes. Solution dyeing was developed to correct this problem in 1951. This process is now possible for all man-made fibers. In 1955, an inhibitor was developed that gave greatly improved protection to the dyes under all conditions that cause fading. However, fume fading can still be a problem.

Acetate fabrics have a luxurious feel and appearance as well as excellent drapability. They are economical.

PRODUCTION

In 1960, six companies were producing acetate; in 1986 there were two: Celanese and Eastman. The basic steps in the manufacturing process are listed in the following chart.

Manufacturing Process

Acetate
1. Purified cellulose from wood pulp or cotton linters
2. Mixed with glacial acetic acid, acetic anhydride, and a catalyst
3. Aged 20 hours—partial hydrolysis occurs
4. Precipitated as acid-resin flakes
5. Flakes dissolved in acetone
6. Solution is filtered
7. Spinning solution extruded in column of warm air. Solvent recovered (see Fig. 10–1)
8. Filaments are stretched a bit and wound onto beams, cones, or bobbins ready for use

Triacetate was produced by Celanese until the end of 1986, when their last triacetate plant was closed. Some triacetate is imported into the United States, so it is important for consumers to be aware that triacetate is a thermoplastic

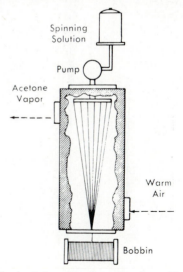

Fig. 10–1 *Acetate spinning chamber. (Courtesy of Tennessee Eastman Co.)*

fiber. It can be heat set for resiliency and dimensional stability. Thus it is a machine-washable fiber.

PHYSICAL STRUCTURE

Acetate is produced as staple or filament. Much more filament is produced because of its silk-like end use. Staple fibers are crimped and usually blended with other fibers. The cross-section of acetate is lobular or flower-petal shaped. (Lobular shape is characteristic of silk-like fibers.) The shape results from the evaporation of the solvent as the fiber solidifies in spinning. Notice in Figure 10–2 that one of the lobes shows up as a false lumen.

The cross-sectional shape can be varied. Y-shaped fibers have been produced for fiberfill for pillows and battings; flat filaments have been produced to give glitter to fabrics.

CHEMICAL COMPOSITION AND MOLECULAR ARRANGEMENT

Acetate—a manufactured fiber in which the fiber-forming substance is cellulose acetate. Where not less than 92 percent of the hydroxyl groups are acetylated, the term triacetate may be used as a generic description of the fiber.—Federal Trade Commission.

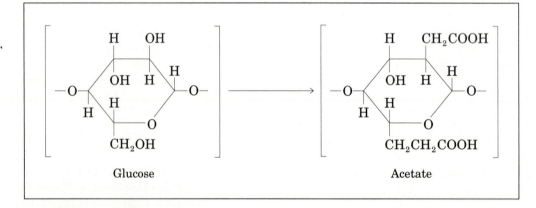

Glucose   Acetate

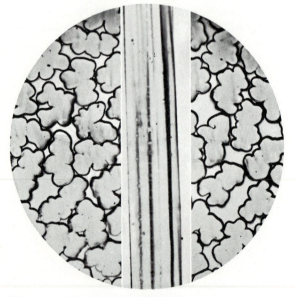

Fig. 10–2 *Photomicrographs of acetate fiber: longitudinal and cross-sectional views. (Courtesy of E. I. du Pont de Nemours & Company.)*

Acetate is an ester of cellulose and therefore has a different chemical structure than rayon or cotton. In acetate, two of the hydroxyl groups have been replaced by acetyl groups. The bulky acetyl groups tend to keep the molecules apart so they do not pack into regions of regularity (crystalline areas). There is less attraction between the molecular chains as a result of a lack of hydrogen bonding. Water molecules do not penetrate as readily, which accounts for the lower absorbency of acetate. The changed chemical structure also explains the different dye affinity of acetate. Acetate is thermoplastic.

PROPERTIES

Acetate has a combination of properties that make it a valuable textile fiber. It is low in cost and has natural body to give it good draping qualities.

Summary of the Performance of Acetate in Apparel Fabrics

AESTHETIC	*EXCELLENT*
Luster	High
Drape	High
Texture	Smooth
Hand	Smooth
DURABILITY	*LOW*
Abrasion resistance	Low
Tenacity	Low
Elongation	Moderate
COMFORT	*MODERATE*
Absorbency	Moderate
Thermal retention	Moderate
APPEARANCE RETENTION	*LOW*
Resiliency	Low
Dimensional stability	Moderate
Elastic recovery	Low
RECOMMENDED CARE	*DRY CLEAN*

Aesthetics. Acetate has been promoted as the beauty fiber. It is widely used in satins, brocades, and taffetas in which luster, body, and beauty of fabric are more important than durability or ease of care. Acetate has, and keeps, a good white color. This is one of its advantages over silk, which yellows readily.

Durability. Acetate is a weak fiber having a breaking tenacity of 1.2–1.4 g/d. It loses some strength when wet. Other weak fibers have some compensating factor, such as good elastic recovery in wool or spandex, but acetate does not. Acetate has a breaking elongation of 25 percent. Acetate also has poor resistance to abrasion. A small percentage of nylon is often combined with acetate to make a stronger fabric.

Comfort. Acetate has a moisture regain of 6.0 percent and is subject to static buildup.

Appearance Retention. Acetate fabrics are not very resilient. They wrinkle as they are worn. When the fabrics are washed, they often develop wrinkles that are difficult to remove. Acetate has moderate dimensional stability. The fibers are weaker when wet and can be shrunk by too much heat. Elastic recovery is low, 58 percent.

Care. Acetate should be dry cleaned unless other care procedures are recommended on the label of the garment. Acetate is resistant to weak acids and to alkalis. It can be bleached with hypochlorite or peroxide bleaches. Acetate is soluble in acetone. Acetate cannot be heat-set at a temperature high enough to give permanent shape to fabrics or to insure that embossing is durable.

Acetate is thermoplastic and heat sensitive; it becomes sticky at 177–191°C (350–375°F) and melts at 230°C (446°F). Figure 10–3 shows two fabrics, one acetate and the other triacetate, which were pressed with an iron set at cotton setting. The acetate fabric softened and shrank, whereas the triacetate fabric showed only a slight imprint of the iron. Triacetate has a higher melting point than acetate.

Acetate has better sunlight resistance than silk or nylon but less than the cellulose fibers. It is resistant to moths, mildew, and bacteria.

Fiber Identification. The *acetone test* is a specific identification test for acetate. None of the other fibers will dissolve in acetone. Figure 10–4 shows a procedure for testing the acetate content of a fabric. Use a dropper bottle, glass rod, watch glass, and cleaning tissue. Test individual yarns first. The presence of other fibers, in blends or combinations with acetate, can be determined. The structure will not disintegrate if

Fig. 10–3 *Effect of heat on (1.) triacetate and (2.) acetate*

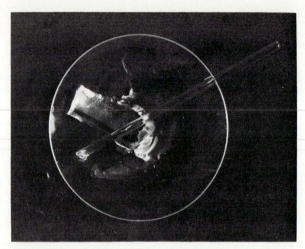

Fig. 10–4 Acetone test for identification of acetate fiber.

only a small amount of acetate is present, but it will feel sticky and will stiffen permanently when the solvent evaporates.

The burning test will also identify acetate. Acetate gives off an acetic—vinegar-like—odor that is specific for acetate. It burns freely, melts, and then decomposes to a black char. Fire-resistant fiber types have been developed.

Comparison With Rayon. Rayon and acetate are the two oldest man-made fibers and have been produced in large quantities, filling a very important need for less-expensive fibers in the textile industry. They lack the easy care, resilience, and strength of the synthetics and have had difficulty competing in uses where these characteristics are important. Rayon and acetate have some similarities because they are made from the same raw material, cellulose. The manufacturing processes differ, so the fibers have many individual characteristics and uses. Some of these are listed in the following table.

USES

Acetate is a minor fiber in terms of usage. Approximately 185 million pounds of acetate were produced in 1984. Americans used about the same amount of wool. Acetate is used in both apparel and home furnishings, but not in industrial products.

The most important use of acetate is in lining fabrics. The aesthetics of acetate—its luster, hand, and body—and its relatively low cost, make it appropriate for this use. However, since acetate is not a durable fiber, the fabric must be carefully selected for the end use or the consumer will be dissatisfied.

The second important use of acetate is in robes and loungewear. It is frequently seen in brushed-tricot and fleece fabrics. In these uses

Comparison of Rayon and Acetate

Rayon	*Acetate*
Differences	
Wet spun	Dry spun
Regenerated cellulose	Chemical derivative of cellulose
Serrated cross-section	Lobular cross-section
More staple produced	More filament produced
Scorches	Melts
High absorbency	Fair absorbency
No static	Static
Not soluble in acetone	Soluble in acetone
Industrial uses—tires	Very few industrial uses
Not used for fiberfill	Used for fiberfill
Color may crock or bleed	Color may fume fade
Mildews	Resists mildew
Moderate cost	Low cost
Similarities	
Low strength	Low strength
Low abrasion resistance	Low abrasion resistance
Chlorine bleaches can be used	Chlorine bleaches can be used
Flammable	Flammable

in the knit structure, the fiber is washable and performs well.

The third important use for acetate is in drapery fabrics. Antique-satin fabrics made of blends of acetate and rayon are very common. They come in an amazingly wide assortment of colors—nearly any décor can be matched. Usually most of the acetate is on the back side of the fabric—the side that faces the window and the sun. Sunlight-resistant variants that can increase the lifetime of the drapery fabrics have been developed. Most of the front side of the fabric is made of rayon yarns and has some textural interest from slub yarns.

The fourth important use of acetate is in fabrics for more-formal wear, such as dresses and blouses. Taffeta, moiré taffeta, satin, and brocade are very common and popular fabrics.

Other important uses of acetate fabrics include bedspreads and quilts, satin sheets, fabrics sold for home sewing, and ribbons.

TYPES AND KINDS

Types of acetate are solution dyed, flame retardant, sunlight resistant, fiberfill, textured filament, modified cross-section, and thick-and-thin slub-like filament.

Types and Kinds of Acetate

Acetate	Trademarks	Producer
Regular	Celanese Acetate	Celanese
	Estron	Eastman
Solution dyed	Celaperm	Celanese
	Chromspun	Eastman
Modified cross-section	Celafil	Celanese
	Celacloud (fiberfill)	Celanese
Textured or crimpable	Celacrimp	Celanese
	Celara	Celanese
	Loftura	Eastman
Combinations		
Acetate/polyester core bulked yarn	Lanese	Celanese
Sunlight and weathering resistant	SLR	Eastman

11

Nylon: The First Synthetic Fiber

Synthetic Fibers

Synthetic fibers are made by putting together simple chemical compounds (monomers) to make a complex chemical compound (polymers). They are also called chemical, or noncellulosic, man-made fibers. The fibers differ in the elements used, the way they are put together as polymers, and the method of spinning used. The synthetic fibers include polyamide, polyacrylic, polyester, polyolefin, polyurethane, and polyvinyl. The synthetic fibers have many properties in common that are listed in the following chart.

COMMON PROPERTIES

Heat Sensitivity. All man-made fibers, except rayon, are heat sensitive. *Heat resistance* is the resistance of a fiber to heat exposure. The term *heat sensitivity* is used with specific meaning for fibers that soften or melt with heat; those that scorch or decompose are described as being heat resistant. Heat sensitivity is important in use and care of fabrics as well as in manufacturing processes. Heat is encountered in washing, ironing, and dry cleaning during use, and in dyeing, scouring, singeing, and other fabric-finishing processes.

The fibers differ in their level of heat resistance. This difference is reflected in the table of safe-ironing temperatures in Chapter 2. The speed of ironing has been found by research to average about 40 inches per minute. This means that in normal ironing the fabric never gets as hot as the sole plate of the iron. If the iron is slowed down or allowed to stand in one spot, the heat will build up. If heat-sensitive fabrics get too hot, the yarns will soften and pressure from the iron will flatten them (Figure 11–1). This flattening will be permanent. Flattening of the

Properties Common to Synthetic Fibers

Properties	Importance to Consumers
Heat sensitive	If iron is too hot, fabric will shrink and then melt. Hole melting from cigarettes. Pleats, creases, and so forth can be heat-set in fabrics. Fabric can be stabilized by heat setting. Yarns can be textured for bulk. Fur-like fabrics can be produced.
Resistant to most chemicals	Can be used in laboratory and work clothing where chemicals are used.
Resistant to moths and fungi	Storage is no problem. Useful in sandbags, fishlines, tenting.
Low moisture absorbency	Products dry quickly. Resist waterborne stains. Stains can be sponged off. Lack comfort in humid weather. Increases possibility of static. Water does not cause shrinkage. Difficult to dye.
Oleophilic	Oil and grease absorbed into the fiber must be removed by dry-cleaning agents.
Electrostatic	Clothes cling to wearer. May cause sparks that can cause explosions or fires. Shocks in cold, dry weather are unpleasant.
Abrasion resistance good to excellent (acrylics lowest)	Good appearance retained longer because holes and worn places do not appear as soon. Color does not wear off as fast.
Strength good to excellent	Strongest fibers make good ropes, belts, and women's hosiery. Resist breaking under stress.
Resilience excellent	Easy-care apparel, packable for travel. Less wrinkling during wear.
Sunlight resistance good to excellent (nylon modified to improve resistance)	Webbing for outdoor furniture. Indoor/outdoor carpet. Curtains and draperies. Flags.
Flame resistance	Varies from poor to excellent. Check individual fibers.
Density or specific gravity	Varies as a group but tend to the lightweight.
Pilling	May occur in staple-length fibers.

Fig. 11–1 *Heat and pressure cause permanent flattening of the yarn (glazing).*

Advantages	Disadvantages
Embossed designs are permanent. Pleats and shape are permanent. Size is stabilized. Pile is crush resistant. Knits do not need to be blocked. Clothing resists wrinkling during wear.	"Set" creases and wrinkles are hard to remove in ironing or in garment alteration. Care must be taken in washing or ironing to prevent the formation of set wrinkles.

surface is called *glazing*. Garment alteration is difficult in heat-sensitive fabrics because creases are hard to press in or out. Fullness cannot be shrunk out of the top of a sleeve or other parts of the garment, so patterns have to be adjusted to remove some of the fullness in areas where fullness is usually controlled by shrinkage.

Heat Setting. *Heat setting* is a factory process that uses heat to stabilize yarns or fabrics made of heat-sensitive fibers. The yarn or fabric is heated to bring it almost to the melting point specific for the fiber being heat set. This temperature range is from 375–445°F. The fiber molecules move freely, dissipating stresses within the fiber. The fabric is kept under tension until it cools, to prevent shrinkage. After cooling, the fabric or yarn will be stable to any heat lower than that at which it was set, but changes can be brought about by higher temperatures. Heat setting may be done at any stage of finishing, depending on the level of heat resistance of the fiber and other qualities. Figure 11–2 illustrates heat setting of flat fabric. Heat setting is both an advantage and disadvantage to the consumer.

Pilling. The strength of fibers is a basic factor in the problem of fabric pilling. *Pilling* is the formation of bunches or balls on the surface of the fabric and occurs on fabrics that have free-fiber ends when the ends get tangled by rubbing. The pills often break off before the garment be-

Fig. 11–2 *Heat-setting nylon fabric.*

comes unsightly, but with nylon and the polyesters the fibers are so strong that few pills break off and they accumulate on the fabric's surface. Pills are of two kinds: lint and fabric. *Lint pills* are more unsightly, because they contain not only fibers from the garment but also fibers picked up in the wash water or through contact with other garments and even through static attraction.

The best single treatment to prevent pilling is *singeing*. Singeing is a necessity for polyester/ cotton and polyester/worsted blends. Singeing consists of running the fabric between two gas flames or two hot plates so it will be singed on both sides at one pass. It should be done very rapidly. The ends of the polyester fibers melt and shrink into the core of the yarn, making it harder for the fibers to work to the surface and form pills. The tips of the fibers look like match heads under the microscope. Singeing should be after dyeing because these fused ends will take a deeper dye.

The construction of the fabric is an important factor in the prevention of pilling. Close weave, high-yarn twist or plied yarns, and longer-staple fibers are recommended. Resin finishes of cotton and fulling of wool are finishes that help prevent pilling.

Static Electricity. Static electricity is generated by the friction of a fabric when it is rubbed against itself or other objects. If the electrical charge is not removed, it builds up on the surface. When the fabric comes in contact with a good conductor, a shock, or transfer, occurs. This transfer may produce sparks that, in a gaseous atmosphere, can cause explosions. Static electricity is always a hazard in such places as dry-cleaning plants and operating rooms. Operating-room personnel are forbidden to wear nylon or polyester uniforms because of the danger. Static tends to build up more rapidly in dry, cold regions. Other problems involving static include

1. Soil and lint cling to the surface of the fabric and dark colors become very unsightly. Brushing simply increases the problem.

2. Dust and dirt are attracted to curtains.

3. Fabrics cling to the machinery at the factory and make cutting and handling very difficult. Static is responsible for increased defects and makes a higher percentage of seconds.

4. Clothes cling to the wearer and cause discomfort and an unsightly appearance. Temporary relief can be obtained by the wearer if a damp sponge or paper towel is wiped across the surface to drain away the static. More-permanent relief can be obtained by the use of fabric softeners. These are effective when used as directed.

Antistatic finishes are applied to many of the fabrics at the factory, but they frequently wash out or come out in dry cleaning.

Oily Stains. Fibers that have low moisture absorption usually have an affinity for oils and greases. They are *oleophilic*. These stains are very difficult to remove and require prespotting with a concentrated liquid soap or a dry-cleaning solvent.

Nylon

Nylon was the first synthetic fiber and the first fiber conceived in the United States. The discovery of nylon was not planned, but resulted from a fundamental research program by Wallace Carothers that was designed to extend basic knowledge of the way in which small molecules are united to form giant molecules or polymers.

In 1928, the du Pont Company decided to establish a fundamental research program. If anything was discovered, it would be good for the company—a means of diversification. The slogan of du Pont is "Better Things for Better Living." Du Pont hired Dr. Carothers, who had done research on high polymers, to direct a team of scientists. These people created many kinds of

polymers, starting with single molecules and building them up into long molecular chains. One of Carothers' assistants noticed that when a glass rod was taken out of one of the polyester stills, the solution adhering to it stretched out into a solid filament. The filament could be stretched even further and it did not go back to its original length. This stimulated the group to concentrate on textile fibers. The polyester they were working on had too low a melting point; the decision was made to concentrate on developing polyamides.

By 1939, du Pont was making a polyamide fiber—nylon 6,6—in a pilot plant. Nylon 6,6 was introduced to the public in women's hosiery where it was an instant success. The term *nylon* was chosen for the fiber. It had no special meaning but had a nice textile sound like cotton and rayon. (At the time there were no laws specifying generic names for fibers. Acetate was still considered a kind of rayon.)

Nylon was called the *Miracle Fiber* for several years. The first thermoplastic fiber ever used, it had a combination of properties unlike any natural or man-made fiber in use in the 1940s. It was stronger and more resistant to abrasion than any fiber; it had excellent elasticity; it could be heat set, and permanent pleats became a reality. For the first time, gossamer-sheer, frilly lingerie was durable and machine washable. Nylon's high strength, light weight, and resistance to sea water made it suitable for ropes, cords, sails, and the like.

As nylon entered more end-use markets, its disadvantages became apparent—static build-up, poor hand, lack of comfort in skin-contact apparel fabrics, and low resistance to sunlight in curtains. But fortunately, as each problem appeared, more was learned about fibers, and ways were found to overcome the disadvantages.

In 1960, five firms in the United States were producing nylon. In 1983, there were nineteen firms in the United States producing nylon: three produced only nylon 6,6; nine produced only nylon 6; and seven produced both nylon 6 and nylon 6,6. Four companies in the last group produced one or two additional nylons as well, including nylon 6,12; nylon 11; or nylon 12.

PRODUCTION

Polyamides are made from various substances. The numbers after nylon indicate the number of

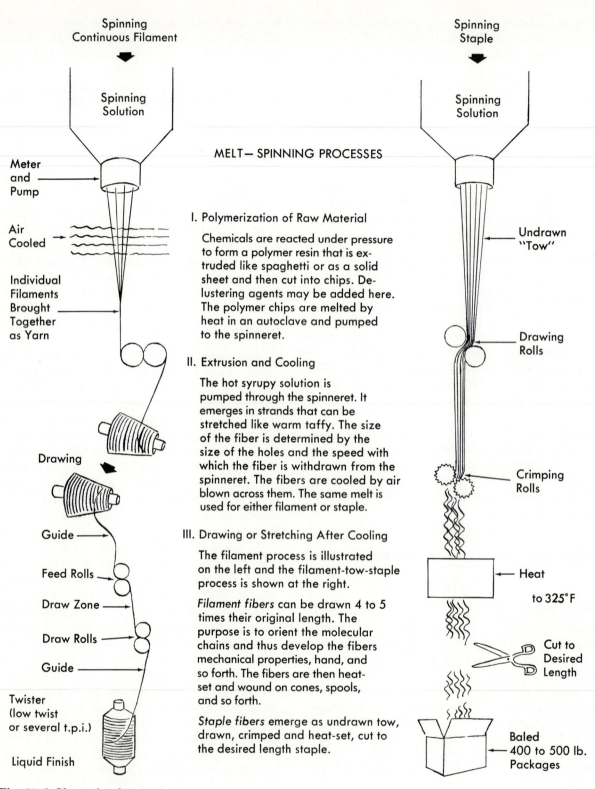

Spinning
Continuous Filament

Spinning
Solution

MELT— SPINNING PROCESSES

Meter
and
Pump

Air
Cooled

Individual
Filaments
Brought
Together
as Yarn

Drawing

Guide

Feed Rolls

Draw Zone

Draw Rolls

Guide

Twister
(low twist
or several t.p.i.)

Liquid Finish

Spinning
Staple

Spinning
Solution

Undrawn
"Tow"

Drawing
Rolls

Crimping
Rolls

Heat
to 325°F

Cut to
Desired
Length

Baled
400 to 500 lb.
Packages

I. Polymerization of Raw Material

Chemicals are reacted under pressure to form a polymer resin that is extruded like spaghetti or as a solid sheet and then cut into chips. Delustering agents may be added here. The polymer chips are melted by heat in an autoclave and pumped to the spinneret.

II. Extrusion and Cooling

The hot syrupy solution is pumped through the spinneret. It emerges in strands that can be stretched like warm taffy. The size of the fiber is determined by the size of the holes and the speed with which the fiber is withdrawn from the spinneret. The fibers are cooled by air blown across them. The same melt is used for either filament or staple.

III. Drawing or Stretching After Cooling

The filament process is illustrated on the left and the filament-tow-staple process is shown at the right.

Filament fibers can be drawn 4 to 5 times their original length. The purpose is to orient the molecular chains and thus develop the fibers mechanical properties, hand, and so forth. The fibers are then heat-set and wound on cones, spools, and so forth.

Staple fibers emerge as undrawn tow, drawn, crimped and heat-set, cut to the desired length staple.

Fig. 11–3 *Chart of melt-spinning processes.*

carbon atoms in the starting materials. Nylon 6,6 is made from hexamethylene diamine, which has six carbon atoms and adipic acid, which has six carbon atoms.

While nylon 6,6 was being developed in the United States, scientists in Germany were working on nylon 6, to which they gave the trade name of Perlon. It is made from a single substance, caprolactam, which has six carbons. Allied and American Enka both began producing nylon 6 in the United States in 1954. In the United States during the 1980s, two-thirds of the nylon produced was nylon 6,6 while the remaining one-third was nylon 6.

Melt Spinning. Nylon is melt spun; this process was developed by du Pont. The basic steps in the melt-spinning process, for both filament and staple fiber made from filaments, are shown in Figure 11–3. *Melt spinning* is essentially a simple process. It can be demonstrated by a laboratory experiment that is fun to do. A flame, a pair of tweezers, and a piece of nylon are all that are needed. Heat the fabric until quite a little melt has formed, then quickly draw out the melt with tweezers as shown in Figure 11–4.

Commercial melt spinning consists of forcing nylon melt through the holes of the stainless-steel plate of a heated spinneret. The fiber cools in contact with the air, solidifies, and is wound on a bobbin. Figure 11–5 shows commercial spinning of nylon as it is extruded through the spinneret into cool air.

The chain-like molecules of the fiber are in an amorphous, or disordered, arrangement and the filament fiber must be *drawn* to develop the desirable properties of the fiber, such as strength, pliability, toughness, and elasticity. Nylon is cold drawn. Drawing aligns the molecules, placing them parallel to one another and bringing them closer together so they are more crystalline and oriented. The fiber is also reduced in size. The amount of draw varies with intended use. The draw ratio determines the decrease in fiber size and the increase in strength.

PHYSICAL STRUCTURE

Nylon is made as multifilaments, monofilaments, staple, and tow in a wide range of deniers and staple lengths. They are produced as bright, semidull, and dull lusters. They vary in degree of polymerization (D. P.) and thus in strength. They are available as partially drawn or completely finished filaments.

Regular nylon has a round cross-section and is perfectly uniform throughout the filament (Figure 11–6). Under the microscope, the fibers look like fine glass rods. They are transparent unless they have been delustered or solution dyed.

At first, the uniformity of nylon filaments was a distinct advantage over the natural fibers—especially silk. Silk hosiery often had rings caused by thicker areas in yarns, which detracted from their beauty. However, the perfect uniformity of nylon produced woven fabrics with

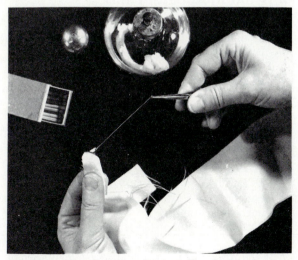

Fig. 11–4 *Spinning a melt-spun fiber by hand.*

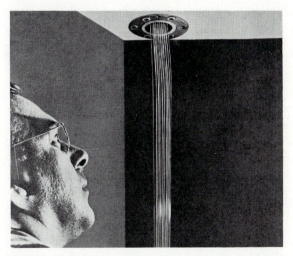

Fig. 11–5 *Spinning nylon fiber. (Courtesy of E. I. du Pont de Nemours & Company.)*

Fig. 11–6 Photomicrographs of nylon fiber: longitudinal and cross-sectional (inset) views. (Courtesy of E. I. du Pont de Nemours & Company.)

a dead feel. They lacked the liveliness of silk. This condition was corrected by changing the shape of the spinneret holes in 1959. Trilobal fibers give a silk-like hand to nylon fabrics (see Fig. 11–7). Qiana is a certification mark used by du Pont for trilobal fibers. In nylon carpets, trilobal fibers and square fibers with voids give good soil-hiding characteristics.

CHEMICAL COMPOSITION AND MOLECULAR ARRANGEMENT

Nylon—a manufactured fiber in which the fiber-forming substance is any long-chain, synthetic

Fig. 11–7 Photomicrograph of trilobal nylon. (Courtesy of E. I. du Pont de Nemours & Company.)

polyamide in which less than 85 percent of the amide linkages $\left[-\underset{\underset{O}{\|}}{C}-NH- \right]$ *are attached directly to two aromatic rings.—Federal Trade Commission.*

The various nylons are all polyamides with recurring amide groups. They all contain the elements carbon, oxygen, nitrogen, and hydrogen. They differ in their chemical arrangement and this accounts for slight differences in properties.

The molecular chains of nylon vary in length. They are long, straight chains with no side chains or crosslinkages. Cold drawing aligns the chains so that they are oriented with the lengthwise direction and are highly crystalline. High-tenacity filaments have a longer chain length than regular nylon. Staple fibers are not cold drawn after spinning and thus have fewer crystallites. They have lower tenacities than filaments.

Nylon has a protein-like molecule and is related chemically to the protein fibers silk and wool. Both have amino dye sites that are important in the reaction of acid dyes. Nylon possesses far fewer dye sites than wool.

PROPERTIES

Aesthetic. Nylon has been very successful in hosiery and in knitted-filament fabrics such as

Summary of the Performance of Nylon in Apparel Fabrics

AESTHETIC	*VARIABLE*
DURABILITY	*EXCELLENT*
Abrasion resistance	Excellent
Tenacity	Excellent
Elongation	High
COMFORT	*LOW*
Absorbency	Low
Thermal retention	Moderate
APPEARANCE	
RETENTION	*HIGH*
Resiliency	High
Dimensional stability	High
Elastic recovery	Excellent
RECOMMENDED CARE	*MACHINE WASH*

Comparison of Nylon 6,6 and Nylon 6

Nylon 6,6	Nylon 6
Made of hexamethylene diamine and adipic acid	Made of captolactam
$$\left[\overset{O}{\underset{\parallel}{C}}(CH_2)_4 \overset{O}{\underset{\parallel}{C}} NH(CH_2)_6 NH \right]_n$$	$$\left[NH(CH_2)_5 \overset{O}{\underset{\parallel}{C}} \right]_n$$
Advantages	*Advantages*
Heat setting 205°C (401°F)	Heat setting 150°C (302°F)
Pleats and creases, can be heat set at higher temperatures	Softening point 220°C (428°F)
Softening point 250°C (482°F)	Better dye affinity than nylon 6,6; takes deeper shades
Difficult to dye	Softer hand
	Greater elasticity, elastic recovery, and fatigue resistance
	Better weathering properties, including better sunlight resistance

tricot and jersey because of its smoothness, light weight, and high strength. The luster of nylon can be selected for the end use—it can be lustrous, semilustrous, or dull. Trilobal nylons have a pleasant luster.

The drape of fabrics made from nylon can be varied, depending largely on the yarn size and fabric structure selected. High-drape fabrics are found in sheer-knit overlays for nightgowns and in sheer-woven overlays in formals. Stiff fabrics are found in taffetas for formal wear or parkas. Very stiff fabrics include webbing for luggage handles and seat belts. These also vary in filament size.

Smooth textures are frequently found. These too can be varied by using spun yarns or by changing the knit or woven structure. The hand frequently associated with nylon fabrics is smooth because of the filament yarn and flat tricot-knit construction. Textured-yarn fabrics are bulkier.

Durability. Nylon has outstanding durability. High-tenacity fibers are used in seat belts, tire cords, ballistic cloth, and other industrial uses. Regular-tenacity fibers are used in apparel.

Tenacity (Grams Per Denier)	Nylon 6,6	Nylon 6
High-tenacity filament	5.9–9.8	6.5–9.0
Regular-tenacity filament	2.3–6.0	4.0–7.2
Staple	2.9–7.2	3.5–7.2
Bulked-continuous filament		2.0–4.0

High-tenacity fibers are stronger, but they have lower elongation than regular-tenacity fibers. During production, the high-tenacity fibers are drawn out more than the regular-tenacity fibers; they are more crystalline and oriented.

Breaking Elongation (Percent)	Nylon 6,6	Nylon 6
High-tenacity filament	15–28	16–20
Regular-tenacity filament	25–65	17–45
Staple	16–75	30–90
Bulked-continuous filament		30–50

In addition to excellent strength and high elongation, nylon has excellent abrasion resistance. Nylon carpet fibers outwear all other fibers.

This combination of properties make nylon the fiber for women's hosiery. No other fiber has been able to compete with nylon in pantyhose. The sheer, almost transparent, fiber is flattering. The fiber is more durable in wear than any other fiber for its sheerness. Filament hosiery develops runs because the fine yarns break and the knit loop is no longer secure. Very sheer hosiery made for evening wear is less durable than the coarser yarn that is intended for daily use.

The high elongation and excellent elastic recovery of nylon account for nylon's outstanding performance in hosiery. Hosiery is subjected to a relatively high degree of elongation; nylon recovers better after high elongation than other fibers do. As it is worn, nylon hosiery recovers its original shape at the knees and ankles, instead of bagging. Another factor that helps it retain its shape during wear is that the shape of hosiery can be pre-set by steaming. The stocking is knit in a tube, then shaped to fit the leg by heat setting the thermoplastic yarns.

Nylon is used for lining fabrics in coats or jackets. A number of years ago, acetate lining fabrics were the most commonly used. They were a poor choice because acetate has low strength and low abrasion resistance. Now nylon linings are available in raincoats, jackets, and winter coats. These linings are more durable.

Nylon is not very durable as a curtain or drapery fabric because it is weakened by the sun.

Comfort. Nylon has low absorbency. Even though its moisture regain is the highest of the synthetic fibers, 4.0–4.5 percent, nylon is not as comfortable a fiber to wear as the natural fibers.

Moisture Regain	Nylon 6,6	Nylon 6
At 70°F, 65 percent relative humidity	4.0–4.5	2.8–5.0
At 70°F, 95 percent relative humidity	6.1–8.0	3.5–8.5

Filament nylon was used in men's woven sports shirts in 1950. The smooth, straight fibers were packed together very compactly in yarns to minimize the transparency of the fiber. This transparency was especially noticeable in light shades when the shirt was wet from perspiration. The yarn and fabric structure resulted in shirts that felt like a plastic sheet wrapped around the body. As the man perspired, the fiber did not absorb the moisture nor did the dense fabric let any moisture escape. The humidity between the skin and the fabric rose, and the person perspired more and became even more uncomfortable. The shirts were especially uncomfortable in warm, humid weather.

Later, fabric structures were made with woven-in open spaces that permitted ventila-
tion. Those were in dress shirts instead of sports shirts so the men were less active. The fabric structure resulted in a more-comfortable shirt.

Because of this early and inappropriate use, nylon got a bad image. On the basis of this experience, fiber producers began to develop fabric quality-control programs through which they could exercise control over the final product and thus protect the image of their fibers. Today, textured and spun yarns used in knit fabrics result in more-comfortable shirts.

Jersey-knit fabrics and tricot-knit fabrics made from nylon are more comfortable than woven-nylon fabrics because the additional air spaces within the fabric structure allow heat and moisture to escape more readily.

The very factors that make nylon uncomfortable under one set of conditions make it very comfortable under a different set. Nylon is widely used for wind-resistant jackets and parkas. The smooth, straight fibers pack closely together into yarns that can be woven into a compact fabric with very little space for wind to penetrate.

Another disadvantage of low absorbency is the development of static electricity by friction at times of low humidity. This disadvantage can be overcome by use of antistatic-type nylon fibers, by antistatic finishes, and by blending with high-absorbency, low-static fibers.

Nylon is very widely used in pantyhose and women's panties. Because of the low absorbency of nylon, doctors recommend that an absorbent crotch panel be used to decrease vaginal irritation and infection. Frequently, cotton is the fiber used for the panel.

Appearance Retention. Nylon fabrics are highly resilient because they are thermoplastic. They resist wrinkling during wear because they have been heat set. The same process can be used to make permanent pleats, creases, and embossed designs that last for the life of the garment. Shrinkage resistance is also high because the heat setting and the low-absorbency fiber are not affected by water.

Elastic recovery is excellent. Nylon recovers fully from 8 percent stretch. No other fiber does as well. At 16 percent elongation, it recovers 91 percent immediately. This property makes nylon an excellent fiber for hosiery, tights, ski pants, and swim suits.

Elastic Recovery	Percent Recovery	At Percent Elongation
High-tenacity	89	3
filament	99–100	2–8
Regular-tenacity	88	3
filament	98–100	1–10
Staple	82	3
	100	2

Nylon does not wrinkle much in use, it is stable, and it has excellent elastic recovery—so it retains its appearance very well during wear.

Care. Nylon introduced the concept of "easy-care" garments. In addition to retaining their appearance and shape during wear, garments made from nylon fabrics retain their appearance and shape during care.

The wet strength of nylon is 80–90 percent of its dry strength. Wet elongation increases slightly. Little swelling occurs in wet fabric made of nylon 6,6. This is in marked contrast to cellulosic fibers. Nylon 6 swells 13–14 percent, cotton swells 40–45 percent and viscose rayon swells 80–110 percent.

To minimize wrinkling, use warm wash water and gentle agitation and spin cycles. Hot water may cause wrinkling in some fabric constructions. Wrinkles set by hot wash water can be permanent. Hot water will remove greasy and oily stains when necessary. Usually the additional wrinkling that occurs in the wash can be pressed out without any problem.

Nylon is a "color scavenger." White and light-colored nylon fabrics pick up color or dirt that is in the wash water. A red sock that loses color into the wash water of a load of whites will turn the white nylon fabrics a dingy pink-gray. This extra color may be so difficult to remove that you may have to resort to color remover. Discolored nylon and grayed or yellowed nylon can be avoided by following correct laundry procedures.

Since nylon has low absorbency, it is quick drying. Travelers find this convenient because items can be hand washed at night and ready to wear the next morning. Because the fabrics are so quick drying, they need to be dried a short time. Do not overdry the fabrics. They can be put in with the rest of the clothes at the beginning of the cycle and removed when dry, or they can be put in near the end of the cycle, or they can be dried on a line.

Dryer temperatures should be warm or low. Avoid using the hot setting on commercial gas dryers. Figure 11–8 is the melted and fused result of a nylon garment dried in an overheated gas dryer with socks of a different fiber content.

Nylon does have problems with static, particularly when the air is not humid, so a fabric softener may be used in the washer or dryer. Nylon should be ironed at a low temperature setting—270–300°F. Home-ironing temperatures are not high enough to press seams, creases, and pleats permanently in home-sewn garments or to press out wrinkles acquired in washing. Using too hot an iron will cause glazing, then melting.

The chemical resistance of nylon is generally good. Nylon has excellent resistance to alkali and chlorine bleaches but is damaged by strong acids. Soot from smoke in industrial cities contains sulfur, which on damp days combines with atmospheric moisture to form an acid that has been responsible for epidemics of runs in stockings. Certain acids, when printed on the fabric, will cause shrinkage that creates a puckered damask effect. Nylon will dissolve in formic acid and phenol.

Nylon is resistant to moths and fungi.

Nylon has low resistance to sunlight. Better resistance is achieved in curtain fabrics by using bright rather than delustered fibers, which absorb rather than reflect light.

Identification. The burning test is one way to identify nylon. Untreated nylon does not flash burn and does not readily support the spread of the flame after the ignition sources are removed.

Fig. 11–8 *The melted and fused remains of nylon garments dried in an overheated gas dryer.*

When exposed to a flame, nylon fuses and draws away from the flame before it will ignite. When it burns, the nylon fibers melt and drip and some of the flame is carried down with the drip. The odor is celery-like, and white smoke is given off. In untreated nylon, the melt will harden as a tan bead. A black bead forms when dyes are present, and certain finishes will increase the flammability.

USES

Nylon is the third most widely used fiber in the United States. It follows polyester and cotton in pounds used and is far ahead of all other fibers. The highest production of nylon occurred in 1979. Since then, total pounds produced have decreased.

Fiber	Million Pounds of Fiber Used (1985)	Percent
Polyester	3,351	30.1
Cotton	2,947	26.5
Nylon	2,379	21.4
Olefin and vinyon	1,239	11.1
Acrylic	644	5.8
Rayon and acetate	558	5.0
Total	11,118	99.9

One estimate for 1986 states that the uses of nylon were as follows:

Home furnishings	60 percent
Apparel	21 percent
Industrial	19 percent

The single most important use of nylon is for carpets. Over 85 percent of the face fibers on carpets in the United States in 1986 were nylon. Tufted carpets are an excellent end use for nylon because of its aesthetic appearance, durability, appearance retention, and ability to be cleaned in place. The combination of nylon fiber and the tufting process resulted in relatively low-cost carpeting that has brought about the widespread use of carpeting in both residential and commercial buildings.

In 1980, 30 percent of nylon went into filament yarns for carpets. Another 23 percent was used in staple-carpet yarns. Thus 53 percent of all nylon produced in the United States was used for carpets. The other 2 percent in home furnishing was used for upholstery fabrics.

The second important use of nylon is for apparel. Lingerie fabrics are an end use for which nylon is the predominant fiber. The knit structure is open enough so the fabrics are comfortable most of the time. The fabrics are attractive and durable; they retain their appearance well and are easy care. Panties, bras, nightgowns, pajamas, and lightweight robes are frequently made from nylon.

Women's sheer hosiery is an important end use of nylon. How frequently they are simply called "nylons"! No other fiber has the combination of properties that make it so ideal for that use. The very sheer hosiery is often 12–15 denier instead of the once standard 30 denier yarn or monofilament. Sheers give the look that is wanted, but they are less durable. Hosiery yarns may be monofilament or multifilament-stretch nylon. They may be plain or textured.

Short socks or knee-high socks are sometimes made from nylon. More frequently they are nylon blends with cotton or acrylic, with the nylon adding strength and stretch.

Active sportswear where comfort stretch is important—leotards, tights, swim suits, and ski wear—is another end use for nylon. Other apparel fabrics are used for blouses and dresses. Nylon-taffeta windbreakers and parkas are commonly seen in cooler weather. Lining fabrics, especially for jackets and coats, are sometimes made of nylon.

Industrial uses for nylon are varied. Within this group, the most important use of nylon is for tire cord. In 1981, 11 percent of the nylon produced was used for this purpose. Nylon is facing stiff competition in this specialized market. It captured the market from high-tenacity rayon, but now may lose the market to polyester, aramid, and/or steel.

Although nylon is strong and abrasion resistant, with high elongation and high elasticity, it has a tendency to "flat spot." Flat spotting occurs when a car has been stationary for some time and a flattened place forms on the tire. The car will have a bumpy ride for the first mile or so until the tire recovers from flattening. With the advent of belted-radial tires and the availability of heat-resistant aramid and steel, the market is changing again. The nylon or polyester fibers that are used in the cord of radial tires go rim to rim over the curve of the tire.

Types and Kinds of Nylon

Cross-Section	Dyeability	Crimp or Textured	Others
Round	Acid dyeable	Mechanical crimp	Antistatic
Heart-shaped	Cationic dyeable	Crimp-set	Soil hiding
Y-shaped	Disperse dyeable	Producer textured	Bicomponent
8-shaped	Deep dye	Undrawn	Faciated
Delta	Solution dye	Partially drawn	Thick and thin
Trilobal	Heather	Steam crimped	Antimicrobial
Triskelion	Optically	Bulked continuous	Sunlight resistant
Trinode	whitened	filament	Flame resistant
Pentagonal		Latent crimp	Delustered
Hollow			High tenacity
			Crosslinked

Car interiors are another example of the varied uses for nylon. The average car uses 25 pounds of fiber, most of which is nylon. Upholstery fabric (called body cloth), carpet for the interior, trunk lining, door and visor trims, head liners on the interior of the car roof, and seatbelt webbing are all nylon fabrics of one kind or another. In addition, clutch pads, brake linings, and yarns to reinforce radiator hoses and other hoses are needed. This again is a very competitive market. Polyester is gaining importance. Research is being done to determine the fiber and fabric structure that is most appropriate for air bags.

Additional industrial uses include the following: parachute fabric, cords and harnesses, glider-tow ropes, ropes and cordage, conveyor belts, fishing nets, mail bags, and webbings.

The category of industrial uses also includes consumer uses and sporting goods. Consumer uses include umbrellas, clotheslines, toothbrush bristles, hair-brush bristles, paint brushes, and luggage. A popular nylon fabric for soft-sided luggage is a 430-denier woven-oxford canvas. In 1986, nylon was used for almost three-fourths of all soft-sided luggage.

Nylon is important in sporting goods. It is used for tents, sleeping bags, spinnaker sails, fishing lines and nets, racket strings, back packs, and duffle bags.

TYPES AND KINDS OF NYLON

It has been said that as soon as a new need arose, a new type of nylon was produced to fill the need. This has led to a large number of types of nylon that are identified by trademarks.

Nearly 200 variants of nylon were listed in the 1983–1984 *Textile Industries* "Man-made Fiber Variant Chart." Differences in luster, denier, mechanical crimp, or staple length were not considered sufficient to define a variant in that list. Over half of the variants of nylon were made by du Pont. Only 8 of the 19 producers of nylon were included in the list. The types and kinds of nylon fibers are too numerous to list as was done for rayon and acetate. The lists on this page illustrate many modifications of nylon.

Some Trademarks and Producers

Nylon 6,6		Nylon 6	
Trade Names	Producer	Trade Names	Producer
Antron, Cantrece, Cordura	du Pont	Anso, Caprolan, Captiva, Hydrofil	Allied
Ultron, Wear-Dated	Monsanto	Natural Touch	BASF Fibers
		Zefran	
		Zefsport	
		Zeftron	
		Shareeen	Courtaulds

12

Polyester

The polyester polymers were part of the high-polymer research program of Wallace Carothers in the early 1930s. When work on the polyesters was discontinued by du Pont in favor of the more-promising nylon fiber, research on polyesters continued in England, and the first polyester fiber, Terylene, was produced there under a patent that controlled the production rights for the world. In 1946, du Pont purchased the exclusive right to produce polyesters in the United States. The du Pont fiber was given the trade name Dacron—a name that is commonly mispronounced. The correct pronunciation is "day'kron."

Polyester was introduced to Americans at a press conference in 1951 where a man's suit was displayed. This suit was still presentable after being worn continuously for 67 days without pressing. It had been dunked in a swimming pool twice and it had been washed by machine. But it had not been pressed. The outstanding resiliency of polyester, whether dry or wet, coupled with its outstanding dimensional stability after heat setting made it an instant favorite.

Dacron was first produced commercially in 1953. In 1958, Kodel, a different kind of polyester, was introduced by Eastman Kodak Company. In 1960, four companies were producing polyester; in 1986, there were 15 producers, including du Pont, BASF Fibers, Celanese, Hoechst, and Avtex Fibers.

Polyester is the most widely used synthetic fiber. Polyester is sometimes referred to as the "workhorse" fiber of the industry. The filament form of the fiber has been said to be the most versatile fiber, and the staple form has been called the "big mixer" because it can be blended with so many other fibers, contributing its good properties to the blend without destroying the desirable properties of the other fiber. Its versatility in blending is one of the unique advantages of polyester.

By the time the polyesters were synthesized, much had been learned about high polymers and about the structure of fibers. Many of the problems of production had been solved—for example, controlled luster and strength, spinning methods, making of tow for staple fibers, and crimping of staple. Continuing research is being done on heat setting, high-temperature dyeing, and static control. Man-made fibers were being promoted vigorously by their trade names. The generic names nylon, rayon, acetate, and acrylic had been agreed on. When the polyesters were introduced, they were backed by quality-control programs that limited the use of a trade name to those products that met standards set by the fiber producers. Consumers readily accepted polyesters.

The polyesters have probably undergone more research and developmental work than any other fiber. The polymer is "endlessly engineerable," and many physical and chemical variations are possible. These modified fibers are designed to improve the original polyester in areas where it has shown either a deficiency or a limitation in its use. One of the important physical changes has been that of changing from the standard round shape to a trilobal cross-section that gives the fiber silk-like properties. A chemical modification, high-tenacity staple, was developed for use in durable-press fabrics. The strength of the polyester reinforces the cotton fibers, which are weakened by the finishing process. Current research is focused on developing a more "natural" polyester—polyester with a hand and absorbency more like the natural fibers.

The properties of polyester that make it the most widely used man-made fiber are listed in the following chart.

PRODUCTION

Polyester is made by reacting dicarboxylic acid with dihydric alcohol. The fibers are melt spun by a process that is very similar to that used to make nylon. The polyester fibers are hot drawn (nylon is cold drawn) to orient the molecules and make significant improvements in strength and elongation, and especially in the stress/strain properties. As the polyester fibers, like the nylons, have the ability to retain the shape of the spinneret hole, modifications in cross-sectional shape are possible.

Figure 12–1 is a diagram of the production of polyester staple fiber. The diagram includes several steps with chips, or small pieces of hardened polymer. Many manufacturers eliminate the chip stage and extrude the polymer directly into fiber.

PHYSICAL STRUCTURE

Polyester fibers are produced in many types—filament yarns, staple fibers, and tow. Filaments

Properties of Polyester

Properties	Importance to Consumers
Resilient—wet and dry	Easy-care apparel, home furnishings, packable garments
Dimensional stability	Machine washable
Resistant to sunlight degradation	Good for curtains and draperies
Durable, abrasion resistant	Industrial uses, sewing thread, good for work clothes
Aesthetics superior to nylon	Blends well with natural or other man-made fibers, good silk-like filaments

are high tenacity or regular, bright or delustered, white or solution dyed. Staple fibers are available in deniers from 1.5–10 and are delustered. They may be regular, low pilling, or high tenacity.

Regular polyester fibers, when seen under the microscope, are so much like nylon that identification is difficult. The smooth rod-like fibers have a circular cross-section (Figure 12–2). The fibers are not as transparent as the nylon fibers.

They are white, so they normally do not need to be bleached. However, whiter types of polyester fibers have been produced by the additon of optical whiteners (fluorescent compounds) to the fiber-spinning solution. The pitted appearance of the Dacron fiber is caused by the delusterant that was added to the spinning solution.

A variety of cross-sectional shapes are produced: round, trilobal, octolobal, oval, hollow, voided, hexalobal, and pentalobal (star-shaped).

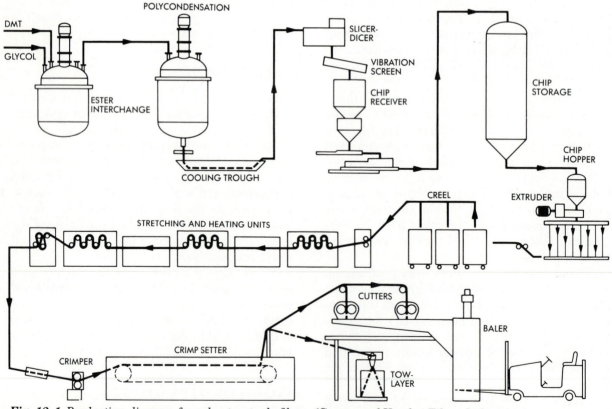

Fig. 12–1 *Production diagram for polyester staple fibers. (Courtesy of Hoechst Fibers Industries.)*

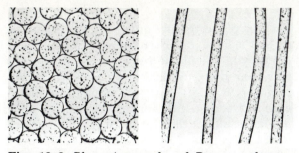

Fig. 12–2 *Photomicrographs of Dacron polyester: cross-section of regular-delustered Dacron 500× (left); longitudinal view 250× (right). (Courtesy of E. I. du Pont de Nemours & Company.)*

CHEMICAL COMPOSITION AND MOLECULAR ARRANGEMENT

Polyester fibers—manufactured fibers in which the fiber-forming substance is any long-chain synthetic polymer composed of at least 85 percent by weight of an ester of a substituted aromatic carboxylic acid, including but not restricted to substituted terephthalate units, $p(-R-O-\underset{O}{\overset{\parallel}{C}}-C_6H_4-\underset{O}{\overset{\parallel}{C}}-O-)$, *and para substituted hydroxybenzoate units,* $p(-R-O-C_6H_4-\underset{O}{\overset{\parallel}{C}}-O-)$.— *Federal Trade Commission.*

Polyester fibers are made from two kinds of terephthalate polymers. The original fibers Terylene and Dacron were spun from polyethylene terephthalate (abbreviated PET). In 1958, Eastman Chemical Products, Inc., introduced a new type of polyester, Kodel, which is spun from 1,4 cyclohexylene-dimethylene terephthalate, commonly known as PCDT. The differences are listed in the following table.

One should not assume from this chart that only Kodel II is low pilling. The PET spinning solutions may be homopolymers or copolymers. The copolymers are pill-resistant, lower-strength staple fibers used primarily in knits and carpets.

Polyester fibers have straight molecular chains that are packed closely together and are well oriented with very strong hydrogen bonds.

PROPERTIES

Polyester fibers are outstanding in their wet and dry resiliency. Because of polyester, ironing has almost been eliminated from apparel and bed and table linens, although many people still do touch-up pressing.

Aesthetic. Polyester fibers accommodate themselves in blends so that a natural-fiber look and

Comparison of PET and PCDT Fibers

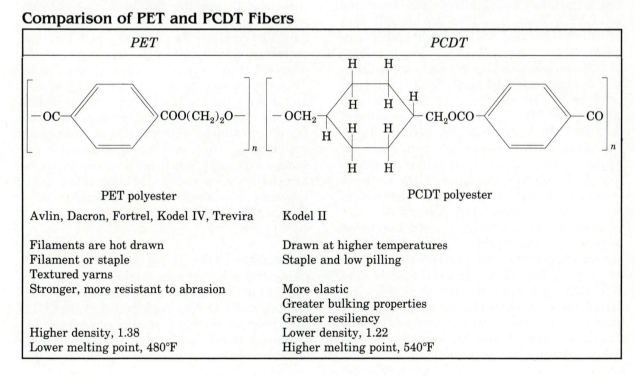

PET	PCDT
PET polyester	PCDT polyester
Avlin, Dacron, Fortrel, Kodel IV, Trevira	Kodel II
Filaments are hot drawn	Drawn at higher temperatures
Filament or staple	Staple and low pilling
Textured yarns	
Stronger, more resistant to abrasion	More elastic
	Greater bulking properties
	Greater resiliency
Higher density, 1.38	Lower density, 1.22
Lower melting point, 480°F	Higher melting point, 540°F

Summary of the Performance of Polyester in Apparel Fabrics

AESTHETIC	VARIABLE
DURABILITY	EXCELLENT
Abrasion resistance	Excellent
Tenacity	Excellent
Elongation	High
COMFORT	LOW
Absorbency	Low
Thermal retention	Moderate
APPEARANCE	
RETENTION	HIGH
Resiliency	Excellent
Dimensional stability	High
Elastic recovery	High
RECOMMENDED CARE	MACHINE WASH

texture are maintained with the advantage of easy care. They are very widely used in blends with cotton for shirts, slacks, and skirts. The appearance of these fabrics is like cotton; their appearance retention during both wear and care strongly proclaims the influence of polyester.

Thick-and-thin yarns of polyester and rayon give a linen-look to summer-weight blouse and suit fabrics. Wool-like fabrics are found in both summer-weight and winter-weight men's suiting fabrics.

Silk-like polyesters have been very satisfactory in appearance and hand. The trilobal polyester fibers were developed as the result of a study by du Pont to find a man-made filament that would have the aesthetic properties of silk. The study, made in cooperation with a silk-finishing company, began by investigating the effect of silk-finishing processes on the aesthetic properties of silk fabrics, since silk seemed to acquire added richness in the fabric form.

In silk fabric, sericin (gum) makes up about 30 percent of the weight. The boil-off finishing process removes the sericin and creates a looser, more-mobile fabric structure. If the fabric is in a relaxed state while the sericin is being removed, the warp yarns take on a high degree of weave crimp. This crimp and the looser fabric structure together create the liveliness and suppleness of silk. The suppleness has been compared to the action of the coil-spring "Slinky"

toy. The properties are quite different when the boil-off is done under tension. The weave crimp is much less, and the response of the fabric is more like that of a flat spring; thus the supple nature is lost. This helps to explain the difference between qualities of silk fabric.

The results of the silk fabric study indicated that the unique properties of silk—liveliness, suppleness, and drape of the fabric; dry "tactile" hand; and good covering power of the yarns—are the result of (1) the triangular-like shape of the silk fiber; (2) the fine denier per filament; (3) the loose, bulky yarn and fabric structure; and (4) a highly crimped fabric structure.

The process was then applied to polyesters. The fibers were spun with a trilobal shape and made into fabrics that were processed by a silk-finishing treatment. The polyesters were particularly suited to this study. They are unique because they can be treated with a caustic soda to dissolve away the surface, leaving a thinner fiber, yarn, or fabric without changing the fiber basically.

Man-made fibers are normally processed under tension by a continuous method rather than by a batch method. Because of the results of the du Pont research study of silk, the trilobal fabrics are processed in a completely relaxed condition. Finishing starts with a heat-setting treatment to stabilize the fabric to controlled width, remove any wrinkles, and impart resistance to wrinkling. The next step is a very important caustic-soda (alkali) treatment, which dissolves away a controlled amount of the fiber. This step is similar to the degumming of silk and it gives the fabric structure greater mobility. All remaining finishes are done with the fabric completely relaxed to get maximum weave-crimp. (Antron nylon is finished in the same way, except that there is no caustic treatment.) Figure 12–3 shows the effect of the alkali treatment on a fabric made of a circular-cross-section polyester.

Durability. The abrasion resistance and strength of polyesters are excellent, and the wet strength is comparable to the dry strength. The high strength is developed by hot-drawing, or stretching, to develop crystallinity and also by increasing the molecular weight. The breaking tenacity of polyester is varied depending on the end use.

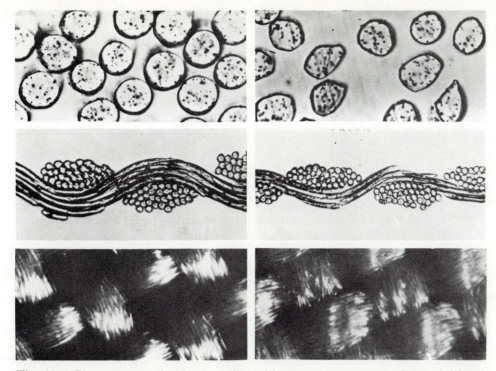

Fig. 12–3 *Photomicrographs showing effect of heat-caustic treatment. Original fabric on left; fabric after treatment on right. Dacron polyester fiber cross-section 1,000× (top); fabric cross-section 200× (center); fabric surface 50× (bottom). (Courtesy of E. I. du Pont de Nemours & Company.)*

Type of Polyester Fiber	g/d	Typical End Use
High-tenacity filament	6.8–9.5	Tire cord, industrial uses
Regular-tenacity filament	2.8–5.6	Apparel and home furnishings
High-tenacity staple	5.8–7.0	Durable-press apparel
Regular-tenacity staple	2.4–5.5	Apparel and home furnishings

Type of Polyester Fiber	Percent Elongation
High-tenacity filament	9–27
Regular-tenacity filament	18–42
High-tenacity staple	24–28
Regular-tenacity staple	40–45

The stronger fibers have been stretched more, so their elongation is lower than the weaker fibers. This is particularly dramatic in the case of partially oriented filament fibers. These are sold to manufacturers who will stretch them more during the production of textured yarns. Their tenacity is 2.0–2.5 g/d. These filament fibers are lower in strength than the staple fibers! Yet their elongation far exceeds that of the other fibers. Their elongation is 120–150 percent! They can be thought of as being partially manufactured fibers until the texturing is completed.

Comfort. Absorbency is quite low for the polyesters, ranging from 0.4–0.8 percent moisture regain. Poor absorbency lowers the comfort factor of skin-contact apparel.

Woven fabrics made from round polyester fibers can be very uncomfortable to wear in warm, humid weather or to wear when the person is perspiring. Moisture does not escape easily from between the skin and the fabric, and the fabric feels slick and clammy.

To increase the comfort of a garment, select a loose-fitting garment design, a thin and somewhat open fabric design, spun rather than filament yarns, trilobal rather than round fibers, and finishes that absorb, or wick, moisture. The soil-release finishes have improved the wicking characteristics of the polyesters, thus improving the breathability and comfort of the fabrics. Additional work on finishes and chemical or fiber modifications is being done in an effort to increase the comfort of polyester.

Blends of polyester/cotton are more comfortable to wear in humid weather than are 100 percent polyester fabrics. Blends of cotton/polyester, where cotton accounts for 60–90 percent of the fabric, are even more comfortable in humid weather. Since cotton is so absorbent, it absorbs most of the moisture. The rest of the moisture is wicked along the outer surface of the polyester fibers to the fabric surface where it evaporates. Polyester is resilient when it is wet, so the fabric does not matt down. Polyester is light in weight and dries quickly.

Polyester exhibits moderate thermal retention. It is generally not as comfortable as wool or acrylic for cold-weather wear. Blends with wool are very successful in increasing its comfort, particularly in men's suits. A lot of work has been done engineering polyester for fiberfill. Fiber modifications—including hollow fibers, binder staple, and crimped fibers—are performing very well.

Polyesters are more *electrostatic* than the other fibers in the heat-sensitive group. Static is characteristic of fibers that have low absorbency. Static is very annoying when it causes clothes to cling to each other. Static is a definite disadvantage because lint is attracted to the surface of fabrics and it is difficult to keep dark-colored fabrics looking neat. Curtains soil more rapidly. New fabrics usually have an antistatic finish, but it is often removed by washing or dry cleaning. The fabric softeners as a laundry aid are good antistatic agents. Temporary relief from static can be gained by running a damp sponge over a garment or by using an antistatic spray. Density of most polyester fibers is 1.38. Hollow variants for fiberfill are less dense.

Appearance Retention. *Resiliency* relates to tensile-work recovery and refers to the extent and manner of recovery from deformation. The following table indicates that polyester has a high recovery when the elongation is low, an important factor in the suiting market. Only small deformations are involved in the wrinkling of a suit, and Dacron recovers better than nylon under those conditions. The recovery behavior of Dacron is similar to that of wool at the

Tensile Recovery from Elongation of:

Fiber	1%	3%	5%	15%
Polyester 56 (regular)	91	76	63	40
Nylon 200 (regular)	81	88	86	77

Source: E. I. du Pont de Nemours & Company, *Technical Bulletin X-142* (September 1961).

higher elongations, which helps explain the compatability of polyester and wool blends. Nylon exhibits better recovery at the higher elongations, so it performs better in garments that are subject to greater elongation—hosiery, for example.

The other polyesters are similar to Dacron in their wet- and dry-wrinkle recovery. This has given them an advantage over wool in tropical suitings, since wool has poor wrinkle recovery when wet. Under conditions of high atmospheric humidity and body perspiration, polyester suits do not shrink and are very resistant to wrinkling. However, when polyester garments do acquire wear wrinkles, as often happens at the waist of a garment where body heat and moisture "set" the wrinkles, pressing is necessary to remove them.

Resiliency and quick drying make the polyesters especially good for fiberfill batts in quilted fabrics—for example, quilts, bedspreads, parkas, and robes.

To summarize, the resiliency of polyester is excellent; it resists wrinkles and, when wrinkled, it recovers well whether wet or dry. Elastic recovery is high for typical apparel items. The dimensional stability of polyester is high. When properly heat set, it retains its size. It can be permanently creased or pleated satisfactorily.

Pilling was a severe problem with fabrics made from the unmodified polyesters. Pilling changes the appearance of fabrics, making them look shabby before they are worn out. Polyester fabrics did not pill more than wool fabrics, but the pills held on and did not break off as they did with wool. Pilling is a problem with all smooth, round fibers of high strength. Low-pilling fiber types have been developed to minimize the problem and to make them more suitable to use in blends with wool and cellulose and in napped and pile fabrics. The finishing process of singeing also helps control pilling of polyester/

cotton blends. Singeing must be done carefully or the fiber ends will appear darker.

Care. Polyester has revolutionized the way Americans care for everyday clothing. White cottons were washed in hot water; colored cottons were washed in warm water. They were dried on a line or in a dryer at a high temperature. Cottons were ironed damp with a hot iron to remove wrinkles. Some people starched their cottons for additional luster and crispness. Clothing was bought large and expected to shrink—especially knit items. Once an item had been worn all day, it looked like it—it was a mass of wrinkles! Wool suits and coats were dry cleaned.

The revolution in clothing care occurred because of the dimensional stability heat setting produces in nylon and polyester fabrics, both knit and woven. Equally important, it occurred because of the advent of durable-press fabrics, notably polyester/cotton blends. During the 1950s and 1960s, cycles on washing machines changed, and special instructions were developed on handling the new durable-press clothing to minimize wrinkling. Now care instructions for polyester/cotton durable-press fabrics can be summarized as follows: Wash in warm water; dry with medium heat in a dryer and remove promptly when the cycle is over; hang; touch-up press with a steam iron.

The excellent abrasion resistance and tenacity, and the high elongation of polyester are unaffected by water; polyester remains the same wet as dry. The low absorbancy of polyester (0.4 percent) means that it resists water-borne stains and is quick to dry. The excellent resiliency of polyester keeps it looking good during wear and minimizes wrinkling during care so only light pressing is required to remove what wrinkles have occurred. Shrinkage resistance is high—indeed, because of heat setting, dimensional stability is excellent.

Warm water is generally recommended to minimize wrinkling of polyester or polyester-blend fabrics. However, hot water (120–140°F) may be needed to remove greasy or oily stains or built-up body soil because polyester is oleophilic, or oil absorbent; polyester has a tendency to retain oily soil. Perhaps one of the most familiar examples of this is "ring around the collar." With polyester shirts or polyester/cotton blends, the soil usually responds to pretreatment, then laundering. If, however, these means are not enough to remove the soil, and it starts to gray the collar in that area, using hot water should help.

Besides holding on to oily soil, another way this can affect laundry results is that soil in the wash water can redeposit on clothing and make it dingy. While polyester is not the color scavenger that nylon is, white polyester will dull or gray if washed with colored or heavily soiled garments. Soil-release finishes applied to fabrics can also make a difference in how well garments clean. The effect of these finishes decreases after many washings.

Another adverse problem of polyester apparel is a tendency to exhibit bacterial odor. Whether or not this is a problem depends on a variety of factors: the person, the fabric, and the laundry procedures. Apparently this is a problem when soil has built up on the fabric; bacteria grow there and an odor results. Use of hot water wash; laundry agents such as borax, which minimizes odor; or bleach to remove the soil buildup and kill the bacteria may minimize the problem. Several detergents were marketed in 1985 and 1986 in response to this problem.

Polyester fibers are generally resistant to both acids and alkalis and can be bleached with either chlorine or oxygen bleaches. This is very important because the largest single use of polyester is in blends with cotton for durable-press fabrics. Polyester fibers are resistant to biological attack and to sunlight damage. The polyester fibers are the most important filaments for sheer curtains.

Polyesters are thermoplastic. They must be heat-set to obtain stability and permanent pleats in garments. Washing in warm water followed by tumble drying is recommended, but polyesters may be safely washed in hot water to remove greasy and oily stains or to remove body oils. Hot water may cause fabrics to wrinkle more and may cause color loss.

The heat properties of the polyesters are used to advantage in the production of fiberfill for pillows, quilts, and linings. The fiber is flattened on one side or made asymmetrical while it is softened by heat, and it will then take on a tight spiral curl of outstanding springiness. Fiberfill can be made of a blend of fiber deniers to give different levels of support for pillows. Lumpiness in pillows can be prevented by spot-welding the fibers to each other by running hot needles through the pillow bat. The snowmobile suits in Figure 12–4 have unquilted nylon shells over Kodel polyester fiberfill insulation.

Identification. The polyesters, like nylon, withdraw from the flame before igniting, so they do not flash burn. They also melt and drip and the flame is carried down with the drip. A black bead forms when the melt hardens. The polyesters can be distinguished from the nylons by odor and smoke. The polyesters have an aromatic odor and produce a heavy black smoke that contains pieces of soot. The fabric must burn briskly before black smoke and soot are evolved, so an adequate sample must be tested to make the identification positive.

USES

Polyester is the most widely used fiber in the United States. Its use has steadily increased since its introduction in 1954. Peak mill consumption of polyester was 3,800 million pounds

Fig. 12–4 *Snowmobile suits with Eastman Kodel polyester fiberfill. (Courtesy of the Rowland Company, Inc.)*

in 1979. Statistics on pounds produced and percent of U.S. mill consumption of polyester are shown in the table.

Year	Million Pounds	Percent of Mill Consumption
1965		4.0
1970	1,600	17.0
1975	3,100	30.0
1980	3,500	31.0
1985	3,351	30.1

Cotton had been the most widely used fiber, but in 1973, 1974, and 1975, cotton and polyester were used almost equally. By 1976, polyester began to be used more than cotton.

Polyester still takes second place to cotton for apparel uses. Of the 4.2 billion pounds of fibers processed for apparel fabrics in 1985, cotton, polyester, and acrylic accounted for almost 88 percent of all apparel fabrics!

Fiber	Percent of Apparel Fabric Fibers Used
Cotton	40.2
Polyester	33.3
Staple	19.2
Filament	14.1
Acrylic	14.2
Other	12.3

Another way of looking at the importance of polyester is seeing the market share it has captured in various markets (see Figure 12–5).

What are the most important uses of polyester? Using data on domestic shipments of yarn in 1984, staple polyester accounted for 64 percent (1,992 million pounds) and filament polyester accounted for 36 percent (1,145 million pounds) of fiber.

Spun Yarns of Polyester Are Used For:

Broadwoven fabrics	1,039.1 million pounds
Fleece and other knit fabrics	283.0
Fiberfill	276.1
Nonwoven fabrics	177.2
Carpet-face yarns	131.4
Pile fabrics	18.4
Blankets	5.5
Other uses	61.3
Total	1,992.0 million pounds